Painless Performance Evaluations

A Practical Approach to Managing Day-to-Day Employee Performance

MARNIE E. GREEN
Management Education Group

PEARSON
Prentice
Hall

Upper Saddle River, New Jersey 07458

Library of Congress Cataloging-in-Publication Data
Green, Marnie E.
    Painless performance evaluations / Marnie E. Green.
        p. cm.
    ISBN 0-13-170675-6
    1. Employees—Rating of. 2. Performance standards. 3. Personnel management. I. Title.
    HF5549.5.R3G62 2005
    658.3'125—dc22

                                                      2005017465

Director of Production and Manufacturing: Bruce Johnson
Senior Acquisitions Editor: Gary Bauer
Editorial Assistant: Jacqueline Knapke
Development Editor: Deborah Hoffman
Marketing Manager: Leigh Ann Sims
Managing Editor—Production: Mary Carnis
Manufacturing Buyer: Ilene Sanford
Production Liaison: Denise Brown
Full-Service Production: Judy Ludowitz/Carlisle Publishers Services
Composition: Carlisle Communications, Ltd.
Senior Design Coordinator/Cover Design: Christopher Weigand
Cover Printer: RR Donnelley & Sons
Printer/Binder: RR Donnelley & Sons

This book was set in GoudyWtcTReg by Carlisle Communications, Ltd. It was printed and bound by
R.R. Donnelley. The cover was printed by R.R. Donnelley.

Pearson Education Ltd.   Pearson Education Australia Pty. Limited
Pearson Education Singapore Pte. Ltd.   Pearson Education North Asia Ltd.
Pearson Education Canada, Ltd.   Pearson Educación de Mexico, S. A. de C.V.
Pearson Education—Japan   Pearson Education Malaysia Pte. Ltd.

10 9 8 7 6 5 4 3 2 1
ISBN: 0-13-170675-6

Dedication

For William L. Finley, otherwise known as Dad,
for giving me the first and best example of what
an effective manager should be.

Contents

Why This Book?

This book is for every supervisor, manager, and executive who has faced a looming deadline of an employee's performance evaluation and wondered, "What should I say?" It is for every supervisor, manager, and executive who has thought, "I have an employee who just isn't 'getting it' and I don't want to talk with them about it." It is for every supervisor, manager, and executive who has said, "I don't have time for all these people issues."

Survey results published in the July 2004 edition of $T+D$ magazine indicated that although almost two-thirds of employees surveyed felt their performance evaluation was accurate, less than a third said it helped them to improve their performance. Most respondents said the reasons for the lack of improved performance included unclear performance goals and not enough honest feedback.

For many reasons, supervisors, managers, and executives find performance evaluations and all the necessary steps that precede them as too time consuming, too awkward, or just not necessary. To those supervisors, managers, and executives: You don't have time NOT to manage performance! The problem is that most managers do not have a system in place to help them conduct this vital management task painlessly. This book provides those tools.

After years of coaching and training supervisors, managers, and executives to better manage employee performance, I have developed a set of tools that can make the process painless. This book is a collection of those tools and a guide for those who are looking for new, more efficient ways to manage performance. Supervisors, managers, and executives around the world who have attended my workshops are using these tools to facilitate better employee communication, improve performance, and ensure better documentation of employee performance.

In addition, human resources (HR) professionals are using these tools to simplify their performance evaluation systems. I offer these ideas to HR practitioners as well, in hopes that their jobs will be made easier through these ideas.

Overall, the goals of this book are to help supervisors, managers, executives, and HR professionals:

- Understand reasons for accurate performance management practices

- Develop mutually agreeable performance goals with each employee

- Use a performance log to document performance

- Document employee performance in a legally defensible manner

- Distinguish between real performance issues and "pet peeves"

- Write clear and accurate comments on the evaluation form

- Establish a work climate that is conducive to productive performance evaluations and focused improved performance

- Initiate and maintain positive communication concerning work performance through documentation and feedback

- Prepare and conduct performance discussions that encourage an exchange of information and produce better results

- Evaluate the employee's performance based on specific, job-related behaviors

- Conduct a productive and painless evaluation meeting with the employee

This book is a collection of ideas, articles, assessments and tools related to the management of performance in the workplace. Pick and choose the concepts and tools that will work for you and develop your own painless approach to performance management.

Best wishes,

Marnie E. Green,
Chandler, Arizona

Acknowledgments

This book is the product of many people's input and guidance. Thanks to the folks at Pearson Education/Prentice Hall for bringing this book to life.

My greatest appreciation goes out to the people who critically reviewed this text as part of the academic review process. Thanks to Charles Greer, M. J. Neeley School of Business, Fort Worth TX; Carol Meyers, Mesa AZ; Denise Gredler, the Gredler Group, AZ; Susan I. Shoemaker, EdD, President, Maximize Potential, Incorporated. You helped me to take the manuscript to another level.

Numerous colleagues contributed to this book by reviewing selected chapters, contributing title ideas, and providing endless support. Many thanks to Kay Wilkinson, Jolaine Jackson, Valerie Rodak, Heather Buckley, Norma Strange, Naney Van Pelt, Greg Eckman, Kathy Miller, Lotus Steers, Liz Harris-Tuck, Bill Stein, Jack Redavid, Vicki Grove, Norm Woodmansee, Brian Boubek, Michael Young, Tom Dorn, Janice Ramirez, Kathy Haake, Fred Bocker, and finally my hiking partner and friend, Dr. Michelle May.

Thanks also to all the managers and supervisors I've worked with over the years who have taught me the difference between good and bad performance management. Special thanks go out to Mike Ingersoll, and Carlos Arauz. You guys set the standard! I'd also like to thank the thousands of supervisors and managers who have attended my workshops and keynote presentations on performance management over the years. Each of you has taught me something by way of your examples and candor.

Mom and Dad, you gave me the confidence to believe in myself at an early age. Thank you for convincing me that I could do anything. This book is a result of your work long ago! And, finally, my love and admiration go out to my husband, Steve Green, who encouraged me to begin writing, was patient with me while I was writing, and who spent hours reading and critiquing the manuscript. Thanks for letting me test out my theories on you!

About Marnie E. Green

With 20 years of human resource development experience in both the public and private sector, Marnie Green is a dynamic and engaging trainer, speaker, facilitator, and author. She designs and leads workshops that dissect the issues facing organizations today. This book, *Painless Performance Evaluations: A Practical Approach to Managing Day-to-Day Employee Performance* offers insights and ideas for those who leave her workshops saying, "I want more!"

As the founder of the Management Education Group, Marnie specializes in designing and delivering organizational development and training solutions that focus on the role of managers and leaders. Leaders are the guiding compass of an organization. The goal of the Management Education Group is to help leaders find their way through the murky waters of working life.

Marnie was instrumental in establishing the City of Tempe, Arizona's Learning Center, the city's virtual corporate university, which provides training and organizational development solutions for the city's 1,500 employees. These solutions included a comprehensive educational partnership with local colleges and universities and an in-depth supervisory development curriculum. While employed by the City of Phoenix, Arizona, Marnie developed, coordinated, and presented supervisory and management academies for thousands of city employees. In addition, Marnie oversaw the implementation of the city's renowned literacy program and developed and presented the citywide ethics program, now used in agencies across the country.

Green's work has been used by organizations in Malaysia, the United Kingdom, Egypt, Costa Rica, and Australia. Her contribution to an international team of consultants with the World Health Organization helped create a cutting-edge organizational change system for the Ministry of Health of several developing countries. These international experiences provide her the opportunity to continually revise and improve her management curriculum to meet the needs of managers throughout the world.

Marnie hold's a Bachelor's degree in Personnel Management and a Master's degree in Business Administration/Finance from Arizona State University. She is a graduate of the Harvard University—Kennedy School of Government Executive Program, The Art and Practice of Leadership Development. Active in several professional associations, Marnie is a member of the American Society for Training and Development and the Society for Human Resource Management, and she has served in leadership roles for the International Public Management Association for Human Resources. She is a frequent speaker at local, national, and international conference on issues related to management and leadership.

For more information about the services of the Management Education Group and the consulting and training services provided by Marnie E. Green contact:

480–705–9394
Management Education Group
1211 North Dustin Lane
Chandler, AZ 85226

E-mail: *mgreen@managementeducationgroup.com*

Website: *www.managementeducationgroup.com*

Introduction to Performance Management

Performance is your reality. Forget everything else.

—Harold Geneen

This chapter will enable you to:

- Define the concept of performance management.
- Explain the many reasons for conducting performance management activities.
- Consider the consequences you and the organization may face if you do not actively manage the performance of employees.

If you've ever wondered how to get employees to do what they need to do, this book is for you. If you've ever stared blankly at performance review forms and wondered where to start, this book is for you. If you've ever struggled with developing clear expectations for others and documenting their results, this book is for you. To manage performance means you are using all the tools available so that you can influence and coach an employee to achieve higher levels of performance and job satisfaction. The term *performance management* may sound complicated, but it's really a fancy way of describing what a good supervisor does. Good supervisors make performance management painless for everyone involved.

IMPORTANT TERM:

Performance management — The process of providing direction, feedback, and recognition to an employee in an organizational setting.

HOT TIP!

Effective performance management leads to clear expectations.

HOW IS PERFORMANCE MANAGEMENT USED ON THE JOB?

The term *performance management* has different meanings to different people. For the purposes of this discussion, performance management is everything a manager or supervisor does to:

- Set clear, job-related expectations

- Provide feedback to employees on how they are progressing toward meeting those expectations

- Complete the organization's required process of regular performance evaluation

Over a ten-year period, the Management Education Group surveyed managers to find out why they thought performance management activities were important. These managers, who came from private, public, and nonprofit organizations, reported numerous benefits to managing employee performance including:

- Setting clear expectations

- Giving feedback

- Determining pay increases

- Documenting successes

- Documenting areas for development

- Facilitating career development and planning

- Enhancing supervisor/employee communication

- Linking day-to-day activities to the organization's strategic goals

- Planning for the organization's future

- Recognizing employee achievements

- Establishing training needs

- Planning for succession

- Defending against legal claims

The reasons we manage performance fall into four main categories:

- *Organizational Objectives*—Effective performance management systems are clearly tied to the goals of the organization and help to support each individual's achievement of those goals. The performance evaluation process is a tool to help employees see how they contribute to the organization's "big picture" objectives.

- *Supervisor/Employee Communication*—If used properly, the performance management process is the primary tool for communication between the supervisor and an employee. As a result, the process can lead to increased morale, trust, motivation, and productivity.

- *Human Resources Activities*—Performance evaluations and the documentation of employee performance is critical to making sound employment-related decisions. Job assignments, promotions, training opportunities, and even termination decisions should be based on job performance. An accurately completed performance documentation provides the basis and the rationale for making these decisions.

- *Legal*—While not the driving factor for a sound performance management process, the final performance evaluation forms and accompanying documentation can and will be used in court proceedings and arbitration hearings should a dispute arise related to an employment decision. Well-documented performance evaluation records can support an employer's "side of the story" if an employment-related decision is challenged.

IMPORTANT TERM:

Performance —
The carrying into execution or action a duty or task; performance is usually measured in achievement or accomplishment, represented by an action. Performance is how the person does his or her job.

THINK ABOUT IT:

Does your organization support the concept of performance management? If so, how?

If your organization supports the concept of performance management, this support is probably indicated through a clear policy and procedure, supervisory and employee training, and leaders who model positive performance management behaviors. If your organization does not support the concept of performance management, you may find that employees do not receive regular feedback about their performance, few records are kept related to employee performance, and employees are not held accountable for their performance.

WHO DRIVES THE PERFORMANCE MANAGEMENT PROCESS?

In short: the employee's immediate supervisor does!

While the human resources department may coordinate the performance evaluation process, each immediate supervisor drives day-to-day performance management activities. Because the overall goal of the performance management process is to improve performance and enhance communication between an employee and his or her supervisor, these tasks and activities cannot be delegated. Only the immediate supervisor can provide the detailed, job-specific, meaningful feedback employees need. If you think this is one thing that can be procrastinated or avoided, you are procrastinating and/or avoiding your job as a supervisor!

In fact, Marcus Buckingham and Curt Coffman, in their book *First, Break All the Rules*, found that exemplary managers surveyed by the Gallup Organization follow a routine when they approach performance management. And, while managers used unique methods to manage day-to-day performance, each manager's performance management routine was simple, frequent, focused on the future, and employee-driven. Top-rated managers required their employees to keep track of their own accomplishments and to share them at each performance review meeting. There is no question, according to the research of the Gallup Organization and Buckingham and Coffman, that the manager is fully responsible for the management of each employee's performance.

HOT TIP!
Establish and follow a performance management routine.

WHY DO SUPERVISORS AVOID THEIR PERFORMANCE MANAGEMENT DUTIES?

While performance management is a necessary and important duty of all supervisors, some supervisors avoid the task. Use the following checklist to determine if you are susceptible to performance management avoidance.

Self-Assessment:

Are you a performance management avoider?

Check any of the items that apply to you:

❏ I don't like judging people. It's like playing God.

❏ I'm afraid that if I address performance, people won't like me.

❏ I end up arguing with my employees about their performance.

❏ I'm afraid my assessments about performance are unfair.

❏ I'm terrible at talking with people about their performance.

❏ I never know if I'm going to get in trouble by saying the wrong thing.

❏ I've never received training on how to evaluate others' performance.

❏ I don't like my organization's performance management forms/system, so I avoid it.

❏ I hate all the paperwork involved with performance evaluations.

❏ No one really values the evaluations, so why should I do them?

❏ I'm not good at keeping performance records on my employees.

THINK ABOUT IT:

If you are a performance management avoider, how does this affect your ability to be effective as a supervisor?

Daily attention to performance management duties, including frequent conversations with employees regarding how they are doing, is critical to a supervisor's success.

WHY IS PERFORMANCE MANAGEMENT SO NECESSARY?

Unfortunately, many supervisors do not perform their performance management duties as diligently as they should. Many of them say they don't understand what the big deal is. They don't have the time to do all that documentation and communication stuff. They have a business, department, school, agency, or organization to run. However you rated yourself on the self-assessment, you are encouraged to consider the great value to you, your employees, and your organization in effectively managing the performance of your staff.

The following real-life case examples illustrate what can happen when performance management duties are ignored. Can you really afford to NOT manage employee performance?

CASE STUDY # 1
PROBATION?

An administrative assistant has been with the organization for a little less than six months. In this organization, employees pass probation and gain certain rights after this six-month "trial" period. After five and one-half months, the administrative assistant's supervisor realizes it is time to complete the evaluation and dreads the task. The employee has not performed up to the supervisor's expectations. The employee is often late to work and has a habit of irritating coworkers with her messy work habits. The supervisor confides in you that he hasn't said anything to the employee during the last five months and is concerned that if he brings these issues up now, he will be in for a battle. He is considering approving the probation and vows to work with the employee, who, he says, "has potential."

- Has this ever happened in your organization?

- What are the potential consequences of letting the employee pass the "trial period"?

- What are the potential consequences of addressing the behaviors at this point?

One hundred percent of the supervisors who reviewed this case example in performance management workshops agreed that this case is a common occurrence. The failure is not on the part of the employee who is not performing to standard. The failure is on the part of the supervisor who did not address the poor performance earlier in the trial period. As a result, most supervisors choose to extend the trial period, hoping the employees will improve. However, this is not an ideal solution, as employees have been deprived of vital feedback early in their career. In the long run, these employees are likely to fail.

The bottom line is that a probationary or trial employee who has been properly trained and coached and who is still unable to perform the job after trial period must be terminated. Hanging on to a poor performer is not fair to the employee and is not good for the organization. In the long run, this kind of poor performance management only results in lower morale and continuing problems in the future.

If that case doesn't sound familiar, see if the next one does.

CASE STUDY # 2
THE INHERITED EMPLOYEE

You are a new supervisor and have inherited an employee who has a reputation for being unproductive. This employee, the clerk in your work unit, is consistently late for work, often calls in sick on Mondays and Fridays, and rarely produces error-free work. You have also heard her being rude to customers on the phone.

Your boss tells you that if her behaviors continue after they have been addressed with her, you should take immediate corrective action to discipline her, up to and including termination. While you want to do all you can to change this employee's behavior, you agree that termination may be an option in the future.

When you take a look at the file left behind by previous supervisors, you find only glowing comments about this employee. Her last three performance evaluations are above average, and none of them mention attendance, accuracy, or rudeness.

■ Has this ever happened in your organization?

■ What predicament might you face if her behavior does not change and you resort to disciplinary action?

■ What are the potential consequences of not addressing the behavior, as it appears the previous supervisors have done?

The amazing thing about this real-life case study is that almost every supervisor who read it said they know this happens in their organization.

Previous supervisors have taken the easy or cowardly way out by avoiding giving constructive feedback to employees. The poor performer is then passed from supervisor to supervisor and begins to believe that the substandard performance is acceptable, or even appreciated. Thus, the cycle continues.

WHAT ARE THE TRENDS IN PERFORMANCE MANAGEMENT?

Recently, several innovations in the area of performance management have surfaced that are making the typical performance management duties less painful. These innovations, which are mostly technological, are helping managers and supervisors carry out their performance management duties more efficiently and effectively. New, web-based products allow managers and employees to establish goals, document progress, and complete quarterly and annual evaluations with the help of an automated system. Software facilitates performance discussions between managers and employees. Because the goal of managing employee performance focuses on outcomes and results, the technology provides the structure that managers need so that they can focus on building a stronger relationship with employees. Such technology is allowing organizations to streamline their performance management process, integrate performance data with other human resource systems like succession plans and pay systems, and better align individual employee goals with company plans. Such systems, called *employee performance management (EPM) software*, are making the supervisor's performance management duties more painless.

Effective supervisors understand the value of managing the day-to-day performance of their employees, whether they use a paper or an electronic system. Performance management activities are essential to achieve organizational objectives, foster employee/supervisor communication, document employment-related activities, and provide documentation should a legal dispute arise.

Performance Checklist

1. Performance management is not about employee discipline; it is about improving performance through feedback, coaching, and training.

2. Performance management is about helping an employee be successful by addressing specific behaviors.

3. Performance management has benefits to the organization, supervisor, employee, and human resources function and for legal purposes.

4. A lack of performance management can impair the organization by retaining employees who should not be retained or by overlooking poor performance when it should be addressed.

5. Performance management is what you get paid to do when you are a supervisor.

What Did You Learn?

TRUE OR FALSE QUESTIONS

Circle T or F to indicate whether each of the following statements is true or false.

T   F   1. Effective performance management results in clear job-related expectations for the employee and the supervisor.

T   F   2. Clearly established training needs are one possible outcome of effectively executed performance evaluations.

T   F   3. Some supervisors avoid effective performance management practices because they are afraid to be honest with their feedback.

T   F   4. The primary reason organizations conduct performance evaluations is for legal purposes.

MULTIPLE CHOICE QUESTIONS

Circle the letter next to the best answer for each question.

1. Which of the following is not a benefit to managing employee performance?
   (a) Linking day-to-day activities to the organization's goals
   (b) Determining pay increases
   (c) Disciplining employees for poor performance
   (d) Enhancing supervisor/employee communication

2. Performance management is everything a supervisor does to help employees by:
   (a) Establishing clear performance expectations
   (b) Giving directions and orders
   (c) Disciplining employees for mistakes
   (d) None of the above

3. Which of the following is *not* a reason for effective performance management?

    (a) Fosters effective supervisor/employee communication

    (b) Allows employees to see the big picture of the organization

    (c) Provides legal documentation of performance

    (d) Creates competition among employees for recognition and rewards

4. Which of the following is a reason some supervisors avoid their performance management duties?

    (a) They are afraid to say the wrong thing.

    (b) They understand the need to be honest with feedback.

    (c) They take full responsibility for the outcomes of their work unit.

    (d) They see a link between their employee's success and their own success.

OBJECTIVE QUESTIONS

1. What recommendations would you make to ensure that your organization encourages supervisors to effectively carry out their performance management duties?

2. What can you do to show your employees that you are taking the job of performance management seriously?

Navigating the Performance Management Process

Dedicate some of your life to others. Your dedication will not be a sacrifice. It will be an exhilarating experience because it is an intense effort applied toward a meaningful end.

—Dr. Thomas Dooley

This chapter will enable you to:

- Implement the suggested model called the *performance management cycle*.
- Explain the roles that supervisors, employees, reviewers, and the human resources department play in managing employee performance.
- Recognize the role of a standardized performance evaluation form.
- Comprehend the link between money and performance management.

Effective performance management is not done just once a year when the human resources department reminds you that an employee's performance evaluation is due. When performance management is effectively carried out, it is a continuous process that supports the organization's goals and strategic initiatives. It is part of every work day, every encounter, and every employee discussion. When seen as a way of doing business, performance management is easy, even painless!

WHAT STEPS SHOULD I TAKE TO EFFECTIVELY MANAGE EMPLOYEE PERFORMANCE?

IMPORTANT TERM:

Performance management cycle—The ongoing process of setting clear expectations, providing ongoing feedback, and documenting an employee's performance.

While every organization has its own forms, timetables, requirements, and expectations related to performance management, some basic principles apply to every system in every organization. While the paperwork may only be required by the organization once a year, performance management is more than paperwork. The performance management cycle is a logical, easy-to-understand model that helps us see the continuous nature of managing employee performance.

Performance management is not something we do TO employees once a year. Performance management is done WITH employees every day. It helps everyone to focus on the organization's goals and how their work contributes to the organization's success. When executed properly, it is an ongoing process of communication and feedback documented in a consistent and legally defensible manner. The diagram on the following page describes the cycle of performance management.

When you are effectively supporting an employee's performance, you are carrying out each stage in the process in the order presented and the employee is involved in each step. Let's explore each step in more detail.

IMPORTANT TERM:

Performance management system—An organization-wide process that establishes and links short- and long-term goals for the organization, for departments, for work units, and for individuals.

Organizational Goals and Strategic Plans

The day to day work performed by employees should support the organization's overall business goals and should link to the strategic direction the organization's leaders have set forth. Generally this means that each employee should understand how his or her contribution furthers the success of the organization now and in the future. This linking of goals is often called the *performance management system.*

Because we live and work in a dynamic and changing environment, the organization's goals and strategic direction may change often. Changes in organizational strategy, budget, structure, and direction should lead to adjustments in the employee's goals and expectations.

THE PERFORMANCE MANAGEMENT CYCLE

Organizational Goals and Strategic Plans

Individual Performance Planning
Employee and supervisor agree on performance goals that support the department's and organization's goals.

Performance Evaluation Discussion
Employee and supervisor meet to discuss performance, evaluate progress, and complete final documents.

Feedback and Adjustment
Employee and supervisor meet frequently, formally and informally, to assess progress and make adjustments.

Performance Evaluation Preparation
Supervisor completes the performance evaluation form based on feedback received and documentation collected.

Documentation
Supervisor documents discussions with employee about progress and changes made to goals.

As a result, effective performance management is an ongoing, flexible process that allows the supervisor and the employee to make adjustments as the organization's needs change.

In addition to reflecting the organization's goals and plans, the employee's goals should also reflect the goals of his or her department. As department goals change, so must the goals and activities of employees. This cascading of goals ensures that employees are contributing to the organization's goals and that workgroups are working together to achieve the challenges set before them. The cascading of organizational goals and strategic plans may look like this:

Individual Performance Planning

In this step, the employee and supervisor agree on performance goals that support the department's and organization's goals. Employees are not mind readers. We can't expect them to fully know our expectations, hopes, goals, and targets without a discussion. At least once a year, if not much more frequently, you and the employee should discuss the expectations for the job and how the expectations relate to the organization's current goals and initiatives. Work goals, organizational objectives, the job description, and quantitative targets may be the focus of this discussion. It is best to document these expectations in some way so that you and the employee can refer to your agreements in the future.

Goals and expectations are not created equally. During this discussion it is appropriate to talk about the priority of the goals so that employees know which goals are the most critical to their individual, as well as to the organization's, success.

Feedback and Adjustment

The employee and supervisor meet frequently, formally and informally, to assess progress and make adjustments. Once employees understand the expectations and goals they are to achieve, they should be given the room to pursue those goals. However, along the way, employees should be recognized regularly for progress they are making. They may need to be redirected or coached if sufficient progress is not being made. They may simply need some daily reinforcement from the supervisor to make sure they are on the right track. These regular discussions are a critical part of successful performance management and may be conducted daily, weekly, or monthly. Most experts agree that performance-related feedback discussions should occur on a quarterly basis at a minimum.

When exceptional performance is noted or improvement is needed, more formal discussions about performance problems should occur throughout this time frame and should be documented on the appropriate forms. Formal discussions that lead to disciplinary action require special attention and should be coordinated with human resources representatives or senior management.

The regular feedback meeting is also the time to make adjustments to the employee's goals that may be necessary due to changes in the organization's strategic goals, availability of resources, or new priorities. As the business environment changes, you and the employee may also find that the employee needs to acquire new skills or competencies to meet changing expectations. Regular feedback meetings ensure that you and the employee are maintaining the needed flexibility to keep up with new demands.

Documentation

The supervisor documents discussions with employees about progress and changes made to goals. After every discussion with employees about issues related to their performance, you should record the essence of the discussion and make note of any changes, agreements, or conclusions that you and the employees have discussed. If the goals or priorities for an employee have changed, you should keep track of these adjustments. Regular record keeping will help you remember the

HOT TIP!

Together with the employee, prepare a document that summarizes your mutual expectations for the employee's performance.

HOT TIP!

Meet with each employee on at least a quarterly basis to discuss his or her performance and to make adjustments to the expectations to reflect strategic organizational changes.

employee's accomplishments and performance challenges, and these notes will be critical in preparing the quarterly and/or annual performance reviews.

Performance Evaluation Preparation

At this stage, the supervisor completes the performance evaluation form based on feedback received and documentation collected. Depending on your organization's process, you will be required to complete a performance evaluation form for the employee on an annual, semiannual, or more frequent basis. This step usually involves completing a form and writing a narrative about the employee's performance. Sample performance evaluation forms are included in the appendix of this book. If you have maintained effective documentation throughout the rating period, this step should be easy. The purpose of the document is to provide a written summary of the employee's achievements and areas for development.

Performance Evaluation Discussion

At this step, employee and supervisor meet to discuss performance, evaluate progress, and complete final documents. Everyone knows the day will come when you must discuss the evaluation with the employee. Many supervisors see this meeting as a confrontation to be dreaded instead of a chance for a productive, forward-thinking discussion. The performance evaluation meeting should be a positive, productive, and future-focused discussion. The discussion should be designed to recognize employees' strengths and to help them build on their successes. It is also a time to develop plans for helping them improve on any areas for development.

> If the appraisal has not been a continuous activity throughout the period, engaging both employee and supervisor, it too easily becomes a "year-end blame allocation" session.
>
> —Robert J. Greene, Ph.D., SPHR, CCP, CBP, GRP

THINK ABOUT IT:

What does the performance management cycle look like in your organization? Is it clearly defined, or do you need to clarify the process? If you need clarification on the performance management cycle in your organization, who would you ask?

The performance management cycle may vary from organization to organization. Some organizations may use a paper-based system to provide feedback. Other organizations use computer-based systems or employee performance management systems to document performance. Your human resources department may be the best resource to better understanding your organization's expectations and processes.

Regardless of the system your organization uses, the steps in the performance management process should be followed. Consider this case study as an example of what can happen when a step in the process is left out.

CASE STUDY # 3
MISSING A STEP

Hannah is a busy supervisor who oversees the work of fifteen operators. She works hard to make sure that she completes each employee's performance evaluation on time, and she meets with each employee once a year to discuss his or her performance and to establish performance goals and expectations for the coming year. In addition, Hannah is busy each day responding to special projects and everyday crises.

Each time Hannah sits down to write a performance evaluation for one of her employees, she struggles to remember the details of the employee's performance. Usually her evaluations are based on what she remembers about the employee most recently. She does her best to give as much detail as possible.

Hannah's employees complain to one another that they do not get enough feedback from their supervisor. One employee recently filed a complaint against Hannah when she received her performance evaluation and was surprised to see that her performance was not up to standard. Hannah was surprised that the employee was surprised.

- What step in the performance management process has Hannah overlooked?

- How does leaving a step out affect Hannah's relationship with her employees?

- What would you recommend to Hannah in this situation?

WHAT ROLES DO THE SUPERVISOR, EMPLOYEE, HUMAN RESOURCES, AND OTHERS PLAY?

For the performance management cycle to be effective, everyone in the organization must play a role. Some players in this cycle may not be obvious. If one player is not performing his or her role effectively, everyone else will feel the effects. The players in this process include:

- The supervisor who carries out day-to-day performance management activities
- The employee
- The supervisor's supervisor, who likely reviews the performance documentation and provides guidance to the supervisor
- The organization's human resources department and staff members
- The organization's leader: CEO, Director, Big Boss

Here is a quick review of the critical roles that each of these players must perform for performance management to be painless for everyone involved.

Role of the Supervisor

Supervisors, those critical people who guide, direct, and support the work of employees, must:

- Communicate the performance management process, including plans for administering the process with employees
- Set crystal clear expectations for the employee's job performance
- Meet regularly with employees to provide feedback
- Fairly and legally document significant events throughout the rating period
- Provide praise often and help motivate employees to achieve expectations
- Correct or redirect behavior when necessary
- Encourage employee growth by teaching, coaching, and mentoring

Role of the Employee

Employees must be accountable for their own performance. These are activities for employees to consider:

- Clarify the expectations for their job with their supervisor
- Ask questions and discuss problems as they arise

- Maintain their own records about their performance
- Share their goals and expectations with their supervisor
- Give input to improve the work environment
- Accept responsibility for their job performance and seek ways to improve it

Role of the Supervisor's Supervisor

The performance management reviewer is usually the supervisor's supervisor. This person should do more than just sign the final evaluation form. To ensure a strong performance management system, reviewers should:

- Ensure consistency in the ratings among those they supervise
- Coach the supervisor when necessary, serving as a sounding board for solutions when the supervisor is handling tough performance issues
- Establish and communicate clear expectations and goals for the work unit
- Ensure the organization's goals and each employee's goals are in sync and complementary throughout the rating period
- Ensure that employees receive feedback in a timely manner

Role of the Organization's Human Resources Department and Its Staff Members

Performance management usually doesn't occur unless a system and/ or structure is in place. Typically, the human resources department will lead this charge with the following roles:

- Offer a performance management system that fits with the organization's culture
- Facilitate the performance management cycle so that the organization's goals are cascaded down to individual goals
- Communicate the system through skill-based training and offer support to supervisors as they use the system
- Maintain up-to-date job descriptions for each job title
- Make adjustments to the system, as needed
- Administer pay increases, bonuses, and other pay and promotional activities

Role of the Organization's Leader: CEO, Director, Big Boss

For an organization to effectively manage day-to-day performance of employees, the leader of the organization must model the principles of performance management. Here are some things that leaders do to show their endorsement of these concepts:

■ Provide and communicate a clear vision of the organization's future, its core values, and its mission

■ Hold other organizational leaders accountable for managing the performance of their direct reports

■ Support the human resources function with time, attention, and resources for activities related to performance management

■ Be a role model of the organization's values

■ Recognize and support those who are good performance managers

HOT TIP!

Conduct a discussion at a staff meeting about each player's role in the performance management cycle to clarify everyone's expectations.

THINK ABOUT IT:

What role do you play in the management of your employee's performance? How could you improve upon the way you carry out your role?

WHAT IF MY ORGANIZATION'S PERFORMANCE MANAGEMENT CYCLE IS DIFFERENT?

Your organization may use variations of the performance management cycle presented here. In some organizations the goals and expectations that are agreed upon between the supervisor and employee reflect the organization's strategic plan or annual performance goals. Some organizations establish goals that are team-oriented or that focus on team performance rather than on individual performance. Others may develop the goals and expectations as a group, and the individual members may share their goals to ensure support and coordination.

Your organization may have other new and creative ways of administering its performance management system. However, the basic principles remain the same: Performance management is about communication, clear expectations, and improving job performance.

WHAT'S THE PERFORMANCE EVALUATION FORM GOT TO DO WITH IT?

Many organizations spend agonizing hours in tedious process discussions designing the perfect performance evaluation form. They debate about whether the form should include prescribed factors to be evaluated or whether the form should allow for a narrative. They argue over whether the rating system should include three levels (Excellent, Standard, Below Standard) or five levels (Far Exceeds Standard, Exceeds Standard, Standard, Below Standard, Far Below Standard). They heatedly discuss the words that will be used to describe the ratings. They list the advantages and disadvantages of having a calculated, numeric overall rating or whether the overall rating should be a subjective assessment of the other factors rated. The debates go on and on.

While the exercise of designing a customized system for each organization has merits, when performance is managed well, the form does not matter. In fact, some organizations have decided that a blank sheet of paper is good enough. As long as the supervisor can write a clear and specific narrative, the blank sheet of paper method may be sufficient. However, your organization has probably provided you with some structure to ensure that the performance feedback employees receive is consistent. You will find several sample performance evaluation forms in the appendix.

The truth is that the format and forms are largely irrelevant. What matters are the tools you and the employee use to communicate about job expectations and employee performance. It's that simple.

WHAT'S MONEY GOT TO DO WITH IT?

Most organizations use their performance management system to determine pay increases. This is a logical connection. But regardless of economics, good performance is the foundation for a strong organization. So, no matter how pay is distributed (pay for performance, team-based pay, bonuses, commission, etc.), the performance of each individual must be monitored, coached, and supported. For that reason, this book will not address compensation issues or how they are best incorporated into a performance management system. Instead, this book will focus solely on performance management. However, if the organization does not carefully manage the system so that compensation and performance management are aligned, there is a risk of creating an environment of favoritism or injustice. Such alignment should be addressed by the organization's leaders and the human resources department.

The management of employee performance, if carried out thoroughly and effectively, will follow a cyclical pattern that starts with clear expectations. Frequent and informal feedback throughout the performance rating time period is critical to ensure clear employee/supervisor communications and to avoid surprises. For this process to function effectively in any organization, the supervisor, the human resources department, the employee, and others play an active role. In the end, each organization may have its own unique process, procedures, and forms. However, the focus of any effective performance management system should be on communicating clear expectations for job performance and on recognizing where performance has met or exceeded expectations.

Performance Checklist

1. Performance management is what we do WITH employees, not TO employees.

2. The performance management cycle indicates that the management of employees is not a once a year activity, but rather a continuous process.

3. Everyone in the organization plays a role in effective performance management.

4. The organization's performance evaluation form and the method for distributing pay increases are largely irrelevant to effective performance management.

What Did You Learn?

TRUE OR FALSE QUESTIONS
Circle T or F to indicate whether each of the following statements is true or false.

T   F   1. Feedback related to performance should be given to the employee at least once per year.

T   F   2. The supervisor is responsible for setting clear expectations for employee performance.

T   F   3. There is one best performance evaluation form that every organization should use.

T   F   4. It is logical to link the outcomes from a performance evaluation to pay increases.

MULTIPLE CHOICE QUESTIONS

Circle the letter next to the best answer for each question.

1. Which of the following is not a step in the performance management cycle?
   (a) Setting clear goals and expectations for performance
   (b) Completing the performance evaluation form
   (c) Discussing the performance evaluation
   (d) Issuing disciplinary notices when necessary

2. The role of the supervisor in the performance management cycle includes:
   (a) Communicating clearly with employees about the performance management cycle
   (b) Meeting once a year to discuss how the employee has performed
   (c) Saving up criticism for the end-of-year evaluation
   (d) None of the above

3. The human resources department must do which of the following to ensure that the performance management cycle is understood:
   (a) Leave the system the same for at least five years to ensure consistency
   (b) Train and support supervisors on how to use the system effectively
   (c) Make sure there is no link between the performance evaluation system and pay
   (d) All of the above

4. The performance evaluation form:
   (a) Must include a three-level rating scale
   (b) Must include a narrative to be written by the supervisor
   (c) Is a critical part of pay/compensation systems
   (d) Is largely irrelevant when compared to the overall purpose of communication

OBJECTIVE QUESTIONS

1. Which phase of the performance management cycle do you do most effectively and why? Which phase could you improve upon and how?

2. The performance management cycle is a continuous process, rather than a once-a-year event. How do you ensure that the continuous nature of performance management is implemented in your organization?

Clarifying Performance Expectations and Setting Goals

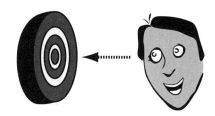

If you don't set goals, you can't regret not reaching them.

—Yogi Berra

This chapter will enable you to:

- Follow a model for establishing clear expectations for others.
- Conduct a future-focused, goal-setting discussion with an employee.
- Establish criteria for setting clear and measurable performance goals.
- Write various goals that might be appropriate for employees.

A Gallup Organization poll of more than 1 million employees and 80,000 managers found that "knowing what is expected" has great impact on employee satisfaction and effectiveness. Effective supervisors know what they expect from their employees, and they communicate those expectations clearly and frequently.

The official job description, usually maintained by the human resources department, is the first place to look when establishing expectations for employee performance. This document should provide an explanation of the basic functions of the job. However, each job and position may require unique expectations that apply to the employee at a certain place or time. The supervisor is responsible for clarifying the job description so that the employee understands it in the context of the job.

> You have to set the tone and pace, define objectives and strategies, demonstrate through personal example what you expect from others.
>
> —Stanley C. Gault

HOW CAN I MAKE MY PERFORMANCE EXPECTATIONS CLEAR?

To make your performance expectations clear, it's important to clearly understand the employee's job and how it relates to the team and the organization. Although your knowledge of each employee's job may be intuitive, take a moment to consider what you understand and expect of each job and of each employee. If you are not clear about how the employee's position contributes to the organization's goals and strategic plan, it will be hard to make your expectations clear to the employee. Consult the job description and discuss the role of the employee and the job with your boss. Take whatever steps are necessary to be clear about the job before you discuss your expectations with the employee.

HOW CAN I HELP THE EMPLOYEE BETTER UNDERSTAND MY EXPECTATIONS?

It is critical that you and the employee are speaking the same language in terms of what is expected. This involves talking about the job and how the employee is expected to perform it. The problem is that many supervisors either don't take the time to have the conversation, or when they do, they don't make their expectations clear enough.

> . . . the majority of problems I see in both professional and personal relationships are due to a lack of clear expectations of all parties, and the rest are due to a lack of accountability to appropriate expectations.
>
> —Susan Scott

THINK ABOUT IT:

When did you ask an employee to do something that you thought was clearly communicated and you got something else? What did you ask for exactly? What did you get instead?

If you are a supervisor, you have likely faced this common dilemma. You ask an employee to complete a task that seems simple to you. What you get is not what you expected. The employee did not complete the job to your standards or expectations. Usually, this frustrating experience occurs when you have not made your expectations clear. You expected one thing and got something else.

Most supervisors have some experience with expecting one thing and getting another. For example, one supervisor described a situation where he asked an employee to "clean out the supply cabinet." The supervisor expected the employee to reorganize the supplies, arrange them in an orderly fashion, and discard any items that were unusable. However, the employee proceeded to empty the entire contents of the supply cabinet and discard all of its contents. When the supervisor checked on the employee's work, he found an empty, yet clean, supply cabinet.

Needless to say, what may seem like an easy or obvious task to one person is not always as obvious to others. These five tips will help make your expectations clear when you are communicating them to an employee.

- *Success Criteria*   Before you turn the employee loose on the task, define the end result as you envision it. By articulating this one idea, you clarify your vision, which increases the likelihood that the employee will see the same end results. You can define success criteria by using the following phrases:
  - "This project/task/job will be successful if _____."
  - "At the end of this task, you will have _____."
  - "The end result should look like _____."

- *Completion Date*   This might sound obvious, but we often forget to share our expectations for when the job should be done. If you expect the task will be done by Friday or by 5:00 P.M. or by the end of the year, say so.

- *Interim Progress or Final Reports*   Just as with the completion date, if you expect an employee to check with you at intervals throughout the task, ask him or her to do so up front. Sometimes asking the employee to check with you periodically can ensure that the employee doesn't go too far down the wrong path.

- *Level of Authority*   Be clear about how far the employee can go in terms of decision making. This will avoid surprises for both of you later on. There are four levels of authority to consider when conveying a task or expectation to an employee:
    - Employee gathers the information, and you make the final decision or carry out the task alone.
    - Employee gathers the information and makes a recommendation, and you make the final decision or carry out the task alone.
    - Employee gathers the information, makes a recommendation, and then with your approval, carries out the task.
    - Employee gathers the information, makes the decision, and carries out the task without your guidance or approval.

- *Areas of Risk or Visibility*   As a supervisor, your job is to give employees all the information they need to do the expected job or task. Sometimes that means giving them a "heads up" as to any areas of potential problems or political sensitivities involved in the job. For example, you might warn them that the project is a high priority for the CEO and the outcome will be carefully scrutinized. Or, if the project is likely to be met by resistance from others, employees should be made aware of these potential challenges. You should help employees find solutions to these issues before they arise, so that they have a greater likelihood of success.

When a supervisor expects something and gets something else from the employee, the cause of the miscommunication can usually be tracked back to one of these factors. Consider this real-life case study to determine where a supervisor could have been clearer.

CASE STUDY # 4
CLEAN SHRIMP

Margaret, a supervisor in the kitchen of a university cafeteria, has just hired a new employee. Michael is a freshman at the university and has taken this job as a way to earn extra money while going to college. On Michael's first day on the job, Margaret asked Michael to "clean the shrimp." She pointed to a pile of raw shrimp on the sink and explained that they would be using the shrimp at an important banquet that evening.

Margaret believes in giving her staff room to do their work. She works hard to avoid micromanaging the employees and when they do a great job, she takes time to praise them. She left Michael for one hour to complete his task.

One hour later she returned to check on Michael. When she asked if he had finished cleaning the shrimp, he said, "Yep, I just finished." Margaret was shocked when she found that half of the shrimp had been cut away, including the tails, and had been thrown into the garbage can. The remaining shrimp had been diced into small pieces, rather than shelled and rinsed as she had expected. Margaret expected that the shrimp would be in whole pieces with the tails still attached so that the cleaned shrimp could be used in the shrimp cocktail that evening.

- Why did Michael misunderstand Margaret's expectations?

- What steps could Margaret have taken to ensure that Michael understood her request?

- How can Margaret ensure that Michael is successful in the future?

THINK ABOUT IT:

Now that you have reviewed the criteria for setting clear expectations, think about the situation you described previously where you expected one thing from an employee and got something else. What could you have done differently in that situation to make your expectations clearer? Which criteria did you leave out?

We never expect to be misunderstood. However, when giving instructions or guidance, it's easy to be unclear about our expectations. These guidelines will help you to be more concise and clear so that the employee can succeed.

WHY DOES MY ORGANIZATION REQUIRE ME TO ESTABLISH WRITTEN GOALS WITH EMPLOYEES?

Performance evaluation expert Dick Grote, author of the *Performance Appraisal Question and Answer Book*, claims that goal setting directly increases productivity. In fact, research has shown that systematic goal setting results in a 39 percent increase in productivity. In organizations

HOT TIP!

Clarify your expectations by asking employees to explain their plan to you before they begin the task.

**IMPORTANT
TERM**

<u>Goal</u>—A job-related
task or activity the
employee is ex-
pected to achieve
that is specific,
measurable, attain-
able, agreed upon,
realistic, and time-
oriented.

where top management showed strong support for individual goal-setting, the productivity increases averaged 57 percent. A systematic and defined goal-setting program is an effective tool for ensuring that the supervisor's expectations for performance are clearly communicated with the employee.

WHAT IS THE BEST WAY TO ESTABLISH GOALS WITH AN EMPLOYEE?

Many organizations' performance management systems require the establishment of goals or objectives for employees. In many cases, these goals are "given" or assigned to employees without their input. Then, when employees do not meet the expectations of the supervisor with respect to the goals, the supervisor wonders why there was a disconnect.

The best way to establish performance goals is with the employee's input, considering the employee's interests, the department's goals, and the organization's goals. By involving employees in the goal-setting process, they will see a more tangible link between their work and that of the organization and as a result will be more engaged. Performance goals should be set *with* employees, not *for* employees. If employees are not full participants in determining the expectations against which they will be evaluated, they are less likely to succeed in achieving them. As a wise saying holds, people support what they help to create.

HOT TIP!

Involve employ-
ees in setting
their perfor-
mance goals.
Ask them for
input.

Here are some tips for developing goals on a mutual basis:

- Offer the employee examples or suggestions of likely goals.

- Give them time to prepare their own goals before you discuss them.

- Ask employees to contribute their goals in writing. Written goals are more "real" than goals that are just in an employee's head.

- Encourage creativity and ownership in the goals.

- Help employees to "stretch" and maximize their individual potential.

- Be prepared for ideas you have not considered. Just because you didn't come up with the goals doesn't mean they are not appropriate or challenging.

- Give employees your full attention when discussing their goals.

> *Define yourself by what you do, by how you treat others, and how they see you. Define your business goals clearly so that others can see them as you do.*
> —George F. Burns

HOW CAN I USE THE SMAART CONCEPT TO SET CLEAR AND MEASURABLE GOALS?

Goals, expectations, and standards are clear when both parties "see" the same end results. A common and often-used tool for creating clear and measurable performance goals is the SMAART acronym. The acronym stands for:

SMAART Goals
S pecific
M easurable
A ttainable
A greed Upon
R ealistic
T ime-oriented

Let's explore each of these concepts to better understand how they lead to clearer goals and expectations.

Specific

Your expectation is crystal clear when you and the employee envision the same end result. When attempting to be clear about your expectations, ask yourself, "What does this activity 'look like' when it is done?" In describing the results expected, you are more likely to completely describe the task or job to the employee.

For example, one manager proposed this objective for an employee:

> Add two new contacts a week from the Healthcare Directory and follow up with them.

From this goal, it would be difficult for the employee to visualize the end result. The expectation is vague and unclear. When the manager was asked what she really wanted from the employee, she explained that there was a monthly trade publication that she expected the employee to read. From the magazine, the employee was expected to identify leads for future business. These leads were to be logged into a database and were

> *Performance objectives are more detailed than the job description and explain specific tasks to be completed.*
>
> —Nicole Alejandre

to be called within one month to make initial contact. She said she expected the employee to call all the leads listed in the magazine.

That much detail was not clear from reading the initial goal, and the employee didn't see it as the supervisor intended. When the goal was rewritten, it looked like this:

> Call every meeting planner listed in the monthly Medical Meetings directory by the end of each month and enter the contact information accurately into the leads database for future follow-up.

The result was a specific expectation that the employee could understand and succeed in accomplishing.

HOT TIP!

Visualize the result and describe it as clearly as possible.

Measurable

For a goal to be complete and understandable, it should also be measurable. Quantitative measures may not always be possible; however, they provide motivation to the employee by identifying a standard. Quantitative measures also provide a benchmark against which the employee's performance can be evaluated.

For example, one supervisor proposed this goal:

> Meet with as many customers as possible each day.

The supervisor was frustrated because the employee was only meeting with two customers a day and the supervisor thought the employee should be doing more. When her manager asked the supervisor how many customers she expected the employee to meet, she said it depended on a lot of factors, including time of year, territory covered, travel time, and availability of customers. After hearing about the job, the manager asked the supervisor one more question: "What is the minimum number of customers the employee should see each day?"

The supervisor replied, "Well, I guess two is what is expected, but three or four would be better." Following this discussion, she settled on this goal:

> Meet with at least two customers per day to provide support and follow-up service as needed.

The supervisor also agreed to talk with the employee to explain that two was the minimum number of customer contacts; to get higher ratings on the performance evaluation, the employee should see three, four, or even five customers per day. The employee appreciated the clarity of the expectation, and the following year, the employee averaged four customer calls per day.

Attainable

Performance goals should be challenging and motivating but not impossible to achieve. Some goals that are intended to challenge the employee to perform to higher levels end up being a frustration for the employee because the goal is inherently unattainable. Unattainable goals are those where the employee does not have the tools, skills, or support to achieve them.

For example, the following goal is probably unattainable for a newly hired checkout clerk at the supermarket:

Check out 300 customers in your four-hour shift with 100% accuracy in your cash drawer.

Most newly hired clerks would not likely be expected to serve 300 customers in four hours. New clerks generally will take a bit longer with each customer to ensure that they are accurate as they are learning the job. However, an experienced checkout clerk may find this target easily attainable. Whether a goal is attainable or not will depend on the expertise and confidence level of the employee, the availability of tools and resources, and the support available.

When you establish goals with employees, be sure to ask these questions:

- What tools will you need to be successful in accomplishing this goal?

- Whose help do you need to complete this goal?

- What resources (time, materials, and money) do you need to accomplish this goal?

If the employee's requests are reasonable and yet cannot be fulfilled, the goal is probably unattainable.

HOT TIP!

Goals should be established so that the employee can find success. Unattainable goals only set the employee up for failure.

Agreed Upon

Both you and the employee should agree upon the goals. If the goals are "given" to the employee without offering the employee an opportunity to provide input or to participate in their creation, the employee is less likely to "buy in" to the goals and thus is less likely to be motivated by the goals.

Realistically, some goals may be part of the organization's overall strategic plan and may be cascaded downward from the top levels of the organization. You can use these as an opportunity to show the employee how his or her work contributes to the big picture. In the best scenario, goals that are handed down create buy-in and commitment.

At the end of the expectation and goal-setting discussion, a document should be created that clarifies the goals and expectations for the coming year. The employee and supervisor can sign this document to indicate that both parties agree to the established goals. The signed document is a good reminder of the commitments made by both parties. The document, which shows the agreements between you and the employee, is not unlike other business contracts. It should clearly describe the agreements you have made in mutual terms.

Realistic

It is common sense that performance goals should be realistic. However, we cannot establish a goal, either for ourselves or for employees, without considering other factors that might come into play while you are trying to achieve it.

For example, in a management team that was working together to establish goals for the coming year, one team member proposed this goal:

> Have a new financial tracking system in place by the end of the year.

All of the team members were excited to hear about the implementation of this new tool.

However, when the director asked a simple question, it made the reality of the situation clear. The director asked, "What are you going to do if the Board does not approve our request for funding of the new system?"

> *Do not put the saddle on the wrong horse.*
>
> —English proverb

The employee who proposed the goal was silent. The director went on to explain that he would love to see the new system put into place by the end of the year. However, if the funding was not approved within the next month, the goal would be impossible to meet. As a result, the goal was modified to:

> Upon approval of funding, implement the new financial management system with roll-out scheduled nine months from the date of the funding approval.

This revised goal reflected the reality of the situation and still allowed the management team to remain focused on the result. The team members agreed to delete the goal from their goal list if the funding was not approved. Everyone was happy and the expectations were clear.

Time-Oriented

Whenever you create a performance goal, always ask yourself, "By when?" Without a deadline or time frame attached to the goal, the employee is left to wonder if time is an issue. Time can be expressed in two ways:

- Deadline—we express deadlines by saying, "by MM/DD/20XX"
- Frequency—we express frequency by saying "daily," "monthly," or "quarterly."

One supervisor wrote a goal for his employee that read:

Complete the sales log in a timely fashion.

He was frustrated because the employee was completing the log inconsistently. When the goal was rewritten, it looked like this:

Complete the daily sales log by 5 P.M. every business day.

This goal made it easier for the supervisor to measure and track the employee's performance, and it helped the employee to better understand the critical nature of the log.

Self-Assessment

Which of the following performance goals are SMAART?

Check the goal statements that follow the SMAART format:

- ❑ 1. Improve the quality of customer service.
- ❑ 2. Reduce the monthly average of products lost in production due to operator error to 5 percent during the next 12 months.
- ❑ 3. Limit the number of customer complaints related to your service to four per year.
- ❑ 4. Complete the performance evaluation forms for each of your employees on or before the scheduled due date.
- ❑ 5. Reduce returned postage charges by 5 percent before May 1.
- ❑ 6. Reduce waste and loss in the company to save money.
- ❑ 7. Try to secure the board's approval for the new computer system by August 15.
- ❑ 8. Promote a more positive work environment by communicating more effectively with your employees.

Of the performance goals listed in the self-assessment, numbers 2, 3, 4, and 5 are SMAART, assuming that the employee performing the goals has the resources and support to achieve them. Goals 1, 6, 7, and 8 are not SMAART. They are not specific, measurable, or time-oriented.

> **THINK ABOUT IT:**
>
> What would be one SMAART goal for an employee you supervise? Be as clear as possible about your expectations of the employee.

Writing SMAART goals is not difficult once you understand the elements of a clearly written goal. Here are examples of performance goals written in the SMAART format:

- Exceed last year's gross sales by 15 percent and establish no fewer than five new accounts by the end of the calendar year.

- By March 10, research, organize, and draft a report on new developments in the plastics industry. Be prepared to share your findings with the entire staff.

- Facilitate the quarterly municipal representative's meeting and report that group's activities at each of our quarterly management team meetings.

- Clean each bathroom thoroughly, including floors, sinks, toilets, and mirrors, by 9:00 p.m. each day.

- Attend a database management class and use the knowledge gained to establish a new database to track our European customers by July 31.

- Make 30 percent fewer data entry errors this quarter as compared to last quarter.

HOT TIP!

Check every performance goal against the SMAART model to ensure that it will be clear and effective.

WHAT KINDS OF ACTIVITIES MAKE EFFECTIVE PERFORMANCE GOALS?

Goals should enhance job performance and should be linked to the organization's strategic direction. Here are four kinds of goals you might consider when setting quarterly or annual performance goals.

1. *"Essence of the Job" Goals*—These goals clearly describe tasks that are required on the job. For example, an accountant might have a goal to prepare and submit monthly financial statements. A library assistant might have a goal to catalogue and reshelf returned books

within two hours of receipt. A mail clerk might have a goal that requires her to deliver all mail daily to all work sites. "Essence of the job" goals make the expectations for the job clearer than they are listed on the job description. These goals personalize the job to the position and to the individual employee. They represent those activities that are most critically important to the job.

Often, employees in the same job type have the same or similar goals. However, it's important to note that employees in the same job or job family may need different goals that reflect the unique complexities of their job assignment. For example, a sales manager in a southern territory may have a different quota than a sales manager in a western territory due to the varying distances they are required to travel. Work with the employee to create goals that are most reflective of their specific job.

> *While many of our work goals are important, only a few qualify as "wildly important." Wildly important goals bring the greatest payback.*
>
> —Stephen R. Covey

THINK ABOUT IT:

What is an "essence of the job" goal that would be appropriate for an employee you supervise?

2. *Project Goals*—Project goals are those activities the employee will pursue that have a beginning and an end and may be above and beyond the employee's routine duties. Project goals may be related to improving systems, developing new products, or creating new programs. Project goals may be activities that are linked to the organization's strategic initiatives, annual corporate goals, and/or department-level goals. Here are a few project goals:

- Create three options for a new design for the product catalog and present your ideas to the board by June 15.

- Develop and present a new customer workshop called "Advanced Applications" by September 30.

- Develop and implement a new electronic filing system for the pending client records by November 15. Ensure that all pending files appear on the "active" list on the day they are due.

- Participate on the organization's diversity team by attending each monthly meeting and by coordinating one diversity-related project for our department by the end of the rating period.

THINK ABOUT IT:

What is a project goal that would be appropriate for an employee you supervise?

3. *Professional Development Goals*—Professional development goals specify what the employee will learn for the coming year. Many supervisors and employees see goal setting as the opportunity to list the classes the employee will attend for the coming year. While learning goals are appropriate, the goal-setting process can be much more meaningful. While attending a class to learn something new is noble, you are challenged to find new ways to help employees develop skills while clearly linking the learning to the organization's needs. Here are a few examples:

OK: Cross train in another work area at least one day a week.

Better: Cross train in the accounting department at least one day a week and be able to cover for the accounting department staff when they are away during each quarterly reporting period.

OK: Attend a training class on PowerPoint.

Better: Attend a training class on PowerPoint and develop a new slide show to be used in new employee orientation by June 30.

It is essential that the professional development goals not only develop the employee, but also relate to the organization's objectives. If the organization needs staff with a certain skill, you may expect employees to be developing competencies related to that needed skill.

THINK ABOUT IT:

What is a profressional development goal that would be appropriate for an employee you supervise?

4. *Performance Improvement Goals*—Performance improvement goals should be saved for those times when you want to clearly emphasize that an employee's behavior must change. Performance improvement goals include things like, "arrive to work ready to serve customers at 8 A.M. every day" or "limit the number of

HOT TIP!

Beware of tasks that look like performance goals. Goals should focus on the outcome of the task rather than the task itself. For example, do not make attendance at a training class a goal. The goal should focus on the result or outcome of attending the class.

customer complaints you receive to three per quarter." Obviously, not all employees require these goals. However, they can be helpful in documenting performance expectations in a clear and measurable way for those employees who are not meeting expectations.

Examples of performance improvement goals include:

- For an employee with poor customer services skills: Answer the telephone within three rings using the standardized greeting provided.

- For an employee who is taking longer-than-expected for breaks and lunches: Return to your desk and be ready to serve customers within 15 minutes after the start of each break and within 30 minutes of the start of your lunch break.

- For an employee who struggles with the timeliness and accuracy of their weekly reports: Submit the weekly report by 4:00 P.M. each Friday and ensure that the data included is error free.

Overall, performance goals should be clear to both the supervisor and the employee as to what needs to be done and how it needs to be accomplished. They should be tangible enough so that everyone can identify whether the goal has been completed or not, and they should be clear enough so that everyone involved can tell whether the goal is being done in an acceptable way. Performance goals should also include a deadline or frequency to indicate when the task should be completed.

THINK ABOUT IT:

What is a performance improvement goal that might be appropriate for an employee you supervise?

Performance Checklist

1. Clear performance expectations are the basis of effective performance management.

2. Employees should participate in the establishment of the performance expectations.

3. Performance goals should be SMAART to ensure clarity and understanding.

4. Written performance goals provide guidance on what employees should be doing and to what extent they should be doing it.

What Did You Learn?

TRUE OR FALSE QUESTIONS
Circle T or F to indicate whether each of the following statements is true or false.

T   F   1. Defining the success criteria of a task can help a supervisor to effectively communicate expectations.

T   F   2. It is not necessary to indicate a completion date for your expectations to be clear.

T   F   3. Every performance goal should be measurable in terms of quantity or quality.

T   F   4. "Essence of the job" goals are the only goals an employee really needs to effectively perform their job.

MULTIPLE CHOICE QUESTIONS
Circle the letter next to the best answer for each question.

1. Which of the following is not an element of SMAART goals?
   (a) Time-oriented
   (b) Action-oriented
   (c) Measurable
   (d) Specific

2. When talking with an employee about possible performance goals, it is important to:
   (a) Ask the employee for ideas of likely goals
   (b) Encourage the employee to stretch in order to maximize his or her potential
   (c) Encourage creativity and ownership
   (d) All of the above

3. Which of the following is the least specific goal?
   (a) Answer the phone within three rings
   (b) Answer the phone each time using the prescribed script
   (c) Answer the phone
   (d) Answer the phone within three rings using the prescribed script

4. Attainable goals are those in which:

   (a) The employee has the tools, time, material, and other resources to be successful

   (b) The employee does not have the understanding and knowledge necessary to finish the goal

   (c) The employee has the knowledge to complete the goal, but not enough time

   (d) None of the above

OBJECTIVE QUESTIONS

1. What benefits do clearly defined expectations and goals provide the employee? The supervisor? The organization?

2. How can goals be used to motivate employees to higher levels of performance?

Documenting Performance Fairly and Legally

Let us take things as we find them: let us not attempt to distort them into what they are not. We cannot make facts.

—John Henry Cardinal Newman

This chapter will enable you to:

- Prepare and maintain complete and detailed documentation about each employee's performance.
- Explore the kinds of documentation supervisors should maintain.
- Use the elements of effective documentation to ensure that your files are complete.
- Implement a tool for effectively documenting day-to-day employee performance.

IMPORTANT
TERM:

Documentation—
The act or an
instance of the
supplying of docu-
ments or supporting
references or
records; confirma-
tion that some fact
or statement is true.

WHY SHOULD I KEEP COMPLETE PERFORMANCE DOCUMENTATION?

Amazingly, many supervisors and managers do not maintain records related to their employees' performance. When an average group of managers was asked by the Management Education Group if they had a file for each employee they supervise, the response was about an 80 percent affirmative response. That means about two out of every ten supervisors have no individual employee records! The obvious question to the 20 percent is: "What do you base the annual evaluation on if you haven't kept records?"

IMPORTANT
TERM:

Recency error—The
tendency to base a
performance
evaluation on the
most recent events
in your memory and
to exclude past
events or incidents
you do not
remember.

Without adequate record keeping, supervisors tend to base performance assessments on memory. Often this leads to the cardinal sin of performance management: the recency error. If assessments about an employee's performance are based on memory alone, there is a tendency to focus on the most recent behaviors and activities rather than on long-term performance. This is not effective because as a result the employee often does not get feedback or recognition for the months of performance that may not have been addressed or documented. If day-to-day performance is discussed and documented, it ensures that neither the supervisor nor the employee will be surprised when a regularly scheduled evaluation is due.

THINK ABOUT IT:

What steps do you take to avoid the recency error when evaluating employee performance? Are your methods effective? Why or why not?

Beyond the need to avoid the recency error, there are many other reasons for continual documentation. Here are a few other reasons why complete and effective documentation is important:

- Documentation records an employee's work history, even if you're not there. When a supervisor gets transferred, promoted, or leaves the job, someone else must take over the supervisory duties. If the previous supervisor does not have adequate records of the employee's performance, the new supervisor must start over.

- Documentation reminds the employee and supervisor of previous conversations. If agreements and commitments are not recorded, it is easy to forget what was agreed upon. Also, if you and the employee agree that the employee is going to change a behavior in some way, and the agreement is not fulfilled, the documentation serves as reminder of the importance of the issue.

- Documentation assists the organization in researching past practices related to discipline. If one employee received a three-day suspension for inappropriate handling of a customer's account, the next employee who commits a similar offense should receive the same discipline. Written documentation offers proof that you and the organization are consistent over time.

- Documentation supports decisions related to employment (promotions, demotions, terminations, training). Fact-based documentation is the best defense for your decisions. If you or the organization is ever challenged about why you promoted one person over another or why you demoted an individual, the documentation should clearly support the decision. The documentation should tell the story for you.

- Documentation facilitates the preparation of the annual performance evaluation. Effective documentation ensures that you include performance examples for an entire rating period rather than for the last few weeks or months. A complete picture of the employee's performance can only be recorded if the documentation spans the entire year or rating period.

Consider this case study as an example of what can happen if a supervisor does not keep adequate documentation on employee performance.

CASE STUDY #5
A BLANK SHEET OF PAPER

David has recently been promoted to the job of manager of the marketing division. Previous to this position, David served as supervisor in the advertising and public relations division. Since these two divisions are closely related, David is familiar with the new employees he will be supervising and he has often worked with them in the past on projects.

In particular, David is familiar with quality of work and work habits of Sam, one of the marketing assistants who now reports to David. Sam has let David down in the past by not meeting deadlines and by preparing less than accurate work. David hopes to be able to address these issues right away and to work with Sam productively in the future.

When David consults the performance file left behind from the previous supervisor, he finds little information. The file includes three past performance evaluations that are short on specifics and long on high ratings. He also finds one note to the file on a yellow sticky note that says, "Need to talk with Sam about deadlines." There is no additional information, no specific situation described, no record that the previous supervisor talked with Sam about his performance. Essentially, the file is as good as a blank sheet of paper.

David is disappointed because he had hoped to be able to pick up where the previous supervisor had left off. He expected to be able to build on the progress the previous supervisor had made in helping Sam to be more effective.

- Can David discuss the past incidents with Sam, based on his own experiences, even if they are not documented by the previous supervisor? Why or why not?

- Where should David begin in terms of the documentation?

- How relevant is David's memory of past incidents to the situation? Can he document his past experiences now?

HOT TIP!

Keep a file folder of documentation for each employee you supervise. This record becomes your working file.

WHAT KINDS OF DOCUMENTATION SHOULD I MAINTAIN?

Supervisors should maintain a working file for every employee they supervise. The working file may be a hard copy file or an electronic file. Many supervisors maintain both forms of documentation. Whatever form you choose to use for your documentation, the documentation should include positive, negative, and neutral examples of the employee's performance. Anything that is factual and representative of the employee's performance should be included in this working file.

Examples of *appropriate* items that are found in the supervisor's working file include:

- Work samples

- Working notes you've made regarding the employee's performance

- Letters of commendation

- E-mails related to work projects

- Certificates of completion from training

- Quantitative records

- Disciplinary notes or forms

- Factual details about work-related incidents

Examples of *inappropriate* items that are sometimes found in the supervisor's working file include:

- Gossip

- Unsubstantiated comments from others

- Personal feelings and opinions

- Accusations that have not been investigated

- Medical diagnoses or summaries of conversations regarding medical conditions

A Painless Reminder

Do **not** put anything in the supervisor's working file that contains medical information. Forward any and all medical documentation to the human resources department, where the staff should maintain a separate medical file for each employee.

In order to comply with the Americans with Disabilities Act, separate medical files should be maintained by the organization for all employees. Medical documentation should not be considered when addressing performance-related issues. And, while physical restrictions and appropriate accommodations must be addressed, they should not be included in the performance file maintained by the supervisor.

The Americans with Disabilities Act (ADA) covers all employers with fifteen or more employees, including state and federal agencies, except private clubs and religious organizations. The ADA is a *nondiscrimination* law rather than an *affirmative action* law, which means that employers must ensure they are not discriminating against those with a real or perceived disability. As a result of the law and subsequent court interpretations, it is critical that organizations keep medical records separate from employment and performance files. The goal is to keep any medical information that could taint a supervisor's view of an employee away from actual performance records. Supervisors should forward all medical documentation to their human resources department.

IMPORTANT TERM:

Americans with Disabilities Act (ADA) of 1990—Title I of the ADA prohibits discrimination in hiring based on disability or perceived disability.

THINK ABOUT IT:

What do your employee files contain right now? What needs to be added or removed?

Using the list of appropriate and inappropriate items listed previously, you should be able to review your files and clean out any information that should not be maintained. If in doubt about whether something should be kept in your file or not, consult your human resources department.

WHAT ARE THE ELEMENTS OF EFFECTIVE DOCUMENTATION?

Not all documentation is created equally. Every piece of documentation should contain these "must-have" elements:

- The current date
- Your name or some way to attribute the information to you
- Factual details, rather than opinions or ideas

Some documentation may be related to more controversial or sensitive topics. When documenting issues related to poor performance or other issues that are likely to have a lingering effect on the organization, remember to also include:

- Purpose of the document
- Who, what, when, where, how
- Statement of the problem
- Reference to related policies
- Reference to past documentation
- Action taken, if any
- Follow-up plans to which you and the employee have agreed
- Signatures from relevant parties
- Employee's response

HOT TIP!

Document **positive and neutral** events, as well as **negative** or **problematic** events!

It is easy to get caught up in documenting a troublesome situation. It is critical that these situations are fairly represented in the employee's file. However, it is important not to overdo documenting these events, and forget to document the good things (or even neutral things) that are happening in the workplace.

Some organizations designate the supervisor's working file as private. In other organizations, like public agencies, the supervisor's working file may be considered a public record and can be seen by anyone who asks to see it. A good rule of thumb is to discuss with the employee everything that is included in the file. If employees were to see their file, they should not be surprised by its contents. This practice ensures that you and employees are discussing all the important issues related to their performance. If it's important enough to put in the working file, it's important enough to discuss with the employee.

HOT TIP!
Do not put anything in the file that has not been discussed with the employee. Remember: No surprises!

WHAT DOES GOOD DOCUMENTATION LOOK LIKE?

Effective documentation can take on many forms. As long as it includes the current date, is attributed to the supervisor, and contains facts, the actual form of the documentation is irrelevant. It can be maintained electronically in performance management software or in a word processing document or spreadsheet. Documentation can be done on sticky notes, on napkins, and on scratch paper. And while these options are a haphazard approach and are not recommended, any format is better than no documentation at all. The best supervisors always have a system for keeping good records about employee performance.

HOT TIP!
Have a system for keeping records about your employees' performance.

Here are a few "best practice" ideas for keeping employee performance documentation:

Record-Keeping Best Practices

- Keep a paper file for those items that come to you in hard copy.
- Keep an electronic file to hold e-mails, work samples, or other pieces of documentation that come to you in electronic form.
- If you use a pencil and paper appointment calendar or an electronic calendar, start recording performance observations in it on the dates they occur.
- Prepare a weekly report on performance observations you've made over the past work days.
- Ask employees to help you keep good records by having them forward regular work updates or a weekly or monthly summary of accomplishments.
- Encourage employees to keep a "me" file where they can keep their own performance records throughout the rating period.
- Maintain a log that reminds you to record the essential elements of good documentation.

HOW CAN A PERFORMANCE LOG MAKE DOCUMENTING EASIER?

The performance log is a great tool to help you remember to document performance and to help you be consistent in your performance notes. The log is a form that gives you a central location for keeping performance notes. The standardized format reminds you of the essential elements of good documentation. The log can be as simple as the following example as seen on page 51.

HOW DO I USE A PERFORMANCE LOG?

The performance log can be your guide to creating legal, fair, and complete documentation. Here are a few tips for putting the performance log to use:

- Put a copy of the log in your hard copy file for each employee and/ or in the electronic file you maintain for each employee. This way, you can enter performance notes in the most convenient form for you.

- At least once a week, enter something about each employee's performance in the log. If you get in the habit of making at least one entry a week—even if the employee has not had a significant achievement or failure during the week—you'll have approximately fifty notes at the end of the year.

- Make notes concerning projects on which the employee has been working. Make notes about specific examples of good performance. Make notes of challenging situations the employee faced. Just make accurate notes!!

- Don't put anything in the log unless the employee is aware of it. The log is not a place to keep your own thoughts. It is a place to record what the employee has been doing and to record conversations you and the employee have that are related to the job. If there is something you think you should write, but you don't want to discuss it with the employee, it's not worth including.

Page 52 includes a sample of the kinds of entries you might expect to make in your performance log.

Your system for keeping performance documentation may be as simple as a file folder or may be as complex as a performance management database provided by your employer. Whatever tools you use, it is crucial that you have a system to record the memorable events of the employee's performance.

PERFORMANCE LOG

Employee Name: _____

Supervisor Name: _____

Date	Situation (Positive, Negative, or Neutral)	Outcome/Result/Action Taken

PERFORMANCE LOG

Employee Name: _Tom Zimmerman_

Supervisor Name: _Elaine Shoemaker_

Date	Situation (Positive, Negative, or Neutral)	Outcome/Result/Action Taken
1/5/xx	_Discussion regarding new job expectations_	_Gave Tom the new job description that was provided by HR_
1/24/xx	_Tom was well received at the progress meeting with the Board. He was organized and to the point with his comments._	_Discussed the presentation after the report Board meeting and told Tom that he did a good job._
1/29/xx	_Tom has been late to the weekly staff meeting for the last three weeks._	_After today's meeting, Tom and I discussed the need for him to arrive on time and he agreed to make it a priority. I explained that when he arrives late, it is disruptive to the team._
2/4/xx	_Tom was late to today's weekly staff meeting._	_I discussed the issue with Tom again and asked him why he was late. He said he got tied up with a customer call. He promised to be on time from now on._
2/16/xx	_Tom has been on time to the last two weekly staff meetings._	_I told Tom that I appreciated his promptness._
3/6/xx	_Received a call from Acme Fence Company's president regarding Tom's customer service. The president said that Tom has gone out of his way to meet their needs and that they are very happy with our services._	_I told Tom about the call and thanked him for his great work. I also sent an e-mail on to Jane (VP) to let her know about the recognition Tom received._
3/15/xx	_Tom submitted the new monthly report on time and completed it as expected._	_No action taken. Report included in this file._

THINK ABOUT IT:

What systems do you currently have in place to document employee performance? What steps can you take now to improve your record-keeping system?

Performance Checklist

1. Documentation is the basis of an effective and fair performance evaluation.

2. Every supervisor should maintain a working file for each employee they supervise.

3. Every piece of information in the working file should be discussed with the employee to ensure that there are no surprises.

4. The performance log is an effective tool for maintaining performance documentation.

What Did You Learn?

TRUE OR FALSE QUESTIONS

Circle T or F to indicate whether each of the following statements is true or false.

T   F   1. Without effective performance documentation, the annual performance evaluation will be based on memory alone.

T   F   2. The performance documentation a supervisor makes is for the supervisor's eyes only. No one else will see those records.

T   F   3. Medical information should be maintained in the supervisor's working file.

T   F   4. Gossip and hearsay are appropriate things to maintain in the supervisor's working file.

MULTIPLE CHOICE QUESTIONS

Circle the letter next to the best answer for each question.

1. Which of the following is not appropriate to keep in the working file?

   (a) Work samples

   (b) Quantitative records

   (c) Personal feelings and observations

   (d) Certificates of completion from training the employee has attended

2. Which of the following are *not* required elements of all effective documentation?

   (a) Signatures from all relevant parties

   (b) The current date

   (c) Your name

   (d) Factual details

3. A performance log is used to:

   (a) Maintain a list of problems the employee is encountering

   (b) Maintain a list of your concerns that are not shared with the employee

   (c) Maintain a record of all relevant performance details that are positive, negative, or neutral

   (d) Maintain your to-do list

4. A system for keeping effective performance documentation may include:

   (a) A paper file folder in the supervisor's desk drawer

   (b) An electronic file

   (c) Notes on a calendar

   (d) All of the above

OBJECTIVE QUESTIONS

1. What are the benefits of keeping complete and thorough performance documentation? What are the risks of not keeping complete documentation?

2. How much detail should performance documentation contain, and how do you know when you have enough?

Making Performance Management a Priority

We must use time as a tool, not as a crutch.

—John F. Kennedy

This chapter will enable you to:

- Incorporate performance management activities into your daily routine.
- Make performance management a priority in your day-to-day work life.
- Use communication tools that support employees in achieving successful job performance.

WHY SHOULD PERFORMANCE MANAGEMENT BE A PRIORITY FOR ME?

HOT TIP!

You don't have time to avoid performance related discussions.

Managers often say, "I don't have time to do this performance management stuff." This statement is most often heard during training sessions on performance management. After considering the critical elements of managing employee performance (clear expectations, frequent and timely communication, fair and legal documentation, appropriate measurements, and objectively written performance evaluations), many managers say, "I'm too busy just doing my day-to-day work! Who has time for all of that?"

You don't have time *not* to manage performance. However, the day-to-day mechanics of managing employee performance can be a little overwhelming. To conquer this challenge, it is important to have a system for keeping in touch with employees about their jobs and their progress. This is not something you can delegate to others.

> **THINK ABOUT IT:**
>
> On a scale of 1 to 5, with 5 being the highest, how would you rate the priority you give to the day-to-day management of employee performance? Why do you rate yourself this way? What does this rating say about your commitment to your employees?

If performance management is not a high priority for you on a daily basis, your employees may not be receiving the support and feedback they need to be effective. The bottom line is that as a supervisor, it is your job to spend time helping your employees be successful.

Consider this case study as you reflect on the importance of making performance management a priority in your daily supervisory activities.

CASE STUDY #6
FINDING TIME TO DO THE RIGHT THING

A manager of a large public relations firm complained that he had too many important things to do and didn't have time to manage performance. During a performance management training session, he said, "I have a great staff and when they have a question, they ask me. If I have a problem with something they are doing, I will let them know. No news from me is good news. I don't have time to chat with each of them and to keep a file documenting everything they do."

After the training the manager's employees were polled about his effectiveness as a leader. More than 90 percent of his staff said he did not fully support them. The staff members said they wished they could count on him for more regular feedback and guidance. They also said they were often unclear about his expectations and they feared they might not do the right thing.

- What impact would regular feedback meetings with employees have on this manager's effectiveness as a leader?

- What can this manager do to help his employees feel they are fully supported?

- How can this manager ensure he has the time to make his performance expectations clear for every employee?

HOW CAN I BECOME A MORE DISCIPLINED PERFORMANCE MANAGER?

Here are a few tips for turning the discipline of managing employee performance into a painless process:

HOT TIP!

Maintain a file folder to hold records confirming each employee's performance.

- *Keep a File for Each Employee*—Unfortunately many supervisors do not have a filing system for keeping performance-related documentation. It's really easy. Just one manila folder with the employee's name on it is all you need! Or, if you choose to use technology, one word processing and/or spreadsheet document will do the trick. These files are essential for keeping the notes, letters of commendation, training certificates, and quantitative performance records that verify the employee's success. If you don't keep these records, who will?

- *Use a Performance Log*—Even if you have a filing system, you may forget to add important things to it on a regular basis. Try using the performance log. Keep one hard copy log for each employee and whenever anything happens that you want to remember (positive, negative, or neutral), make a note on the log. Keep an electronic log, if you prefer, to type your notes rather than write them. If your organization uses an electronic performance management system, a log may be built in for you. You may even set up an electronic log in your PDA so that you can record performance notes while you're on the road. Regardless of the form, the log reminds you to include a date, a detailed description of the event, and any results or outcomes that emerged from the event. Remember, even if you were to make one entry per week in each employee's log, you would have made more than fifty entries per employee by the end of a year. These entries then become the basis for the employee's performance evaluation.

- *Regularly Scheduled Meetings*—This sounds like a simple solution, but many managers say they don't have time to meet on a regular basis with each employee. These are the same managers who struggle with nonperformers and wonder why the employees don't meet their performance expectations. Plan to meet on a regular (weekly, biweekly, or monthly) basis with each employee. This meeting doesn't have to last for more than ten or fifteen minutes. It can be in the office or conducted more informally over lunch or coffee. For remote employees, the conversation may be held over the phone or via teleconference. Discuss the employee's performance plan and solicit input on how the plan is working. This meeting can be used to update and review the employee's progress on performance goals. If you are having these regular meetings, there should be no surprises at the end of the year. If there are no surprises, you are saving time.

> *Weekly or monthly chats with each employee on how things are going can go a long way to building performance management into your routine.*
>
> —Deborah Keary

HOT TIP!

Use your organization's performance evaluation form to keep performance notes. At evaluation time, performance examples are already included in the right places on the form.

- *Use the Performance Evaluation Form to Record Performance Examples*—If your organization has a standard performance evaluation form, electronically save one copy of that form for each employee. As the employee's performance is observed throughout the year, record examples of the performance in the appropriate place on the form. At the end of the year or rating period, when the performance evaluation is due, you will have a head start in making comments on the performance evaluation. Many organizations are converting their performance evaluation systems to electronic forms. Use these tools to capture the highlights and lowlights of each employee's performance along the way.

- *Use Technology*—Today, e-mails provide strong documentation; this is a capability we did not have in the past. In addition to your manila file folder for each employee, keep an electronic folder in which you store e-mails and other electronic documents from and about each employee. If you have an electronic filing system set up on your computer, you are more likely to keep orderly documentation, which leads to more accurate performance tracking. Here are some examples of the kinds of e-mails you might keep in an electronic performance folder:

EXAMPLE EMAIL DOCUMENTATION 1

EXAMPLE EMAIL DOCUMENTATION 2

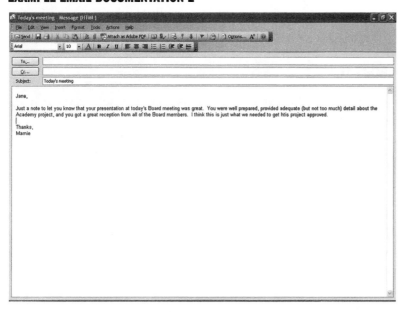

HOW CAN I FOSTER DAY-TO-DAY PERFORMANCE DISCUSSIONS WITH MY EMPLOYEES?

Many supervisors say they do not have time to chat with every employee every day. However, a personal connection each day can provide a supervisor with input on how the work is coming along and gives the employee an opportunity to share concerns and ideas before there is a problem. Day-to-day feedback can be easy if you follow this rule:

Ask two questions of every employee daily.

If you ask two kinds of questions of each employee every day, you'll be miles ahead. Begin these questions with:

"How do you feel?"

and

"What do you need?"

These don't have to be touchy-feely questions. Ask them in relation to the job. "*How do you feel* about the new equipment?" "*What do you need* to produce an error-free report?" By asking these two basic questions, you are communicating to employees that they are valued and their input is heard. When you ask these two questions, the employee's world will open up to you.

> There should be no room for surprises on an annual evaluation report if performance counseling is conducted on its monthly or quarterly schedule.
>
> —Nicole Alejandre

THINK ABOUT IT:

What are one or two things you can implement immediately to show your employees that their performance is important to you?

Most importantly, managing performance means regular communication about expectations, performance, and any gaps that arise. There will always be something to distract you from this important task. However, if you build it into your routine as a manager—having regular, meaningful discussions with each employee—you'll save time in the long run and build stronger employee relationships.

Performance Checklist

1. Performance management duties are a critical part of every supervisor's job.

2. Employees want and need feedback from their supervisors on a regular basis.

3. Effective supervisors use a systematic approach to performance management that includes regular meetings and a consistent format for documentation.

4. Supervising day-to-day employee performance is not an additional job duty—it is the primary role of the supervisor.

What Did You Learn?

TRUE OR FALSE QUESTIONS

Circle T or F to indicate whether each of the following statements is true or false.

T   F   1. Busy supervisors can delegate the task of performance management to others.

T   F   2. Regular meetings related to employee performance must last at least one hour each to be effective.

T   F   3. A supervisor's credibility may be impaired if he or she does not find sufficient time to manage each employee's performance.

T   F   4. Effective performance management means regular communication with employees.

MULTIPLE CHOICE QUESTIONS

Circle the letter next to the best answer for each question.

1. Which of the following is not a way to let employees know their performance is a priority for you?
   (a) Communicate with them only by e-mail.
   (b) Keep a performance log and share its contents with them regularly.
   (c) Schedule a weekly meeting with each employee to review their performance successes and challenges.
   (d) Ask the employee how they feel.

2. Supervisors who don't have time to carry out their performance management duties:

    (a) Are probably not giving enough support and guidance to their employees.

    (b) Don't keep effective documentation of each employee's successes and challenges.

    (c) May lose credibility as a leader of their employees.

    (d) All of the above

3. Which of the following is *not* a way of making performance management a discipline?

    (a) Use technology to keep performance notes.

    (b) Get in the habit of asking each employee how they feel and what they need.

    (c) Perform performance management duties at least one month prior to the employee's annual evaluation.

    (d) Keep a working file for each employee.

4. An effective meeting to discuss an employee's performance:

    (a) Should last at least one hour or more.

    (b) Should focus on disciplining and correcting an employee's behavior.

    (c) Should be avoided unless there are problems with the employee's behavior.

    (d) Should assist in avoiding surprises at the end of the rating period.

OBJECTIVE QUESTIONS

1. How does regular feedback from the supervisor affect overall employee performance? How does it impact employee morale?

2. If a supervisor has not made performance management (regular feedback, clear expectations, sound documentation, etc.) a priority in the past, how can he or she let employees know that these activities are now a priority? Where does the supervisor start?

Identifying and Addressing Performance Issues

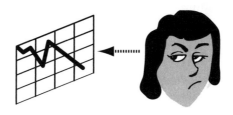

Lucy:	*Do you think anybody ever really changes?*
Linus:	*I've changed a lot in the last year.*
Lucy:	*I mean for the better.*

—Charles Schultz

This chapter will enable you to:

- Assess whether an employee's performance is a legitimate issue to address or a personal pet peeve.

- Differentiate between employee behaviors and attitudes.

- Prepare to conduct a tough performance-related discussion.

- Conduct a performance-related discussion confidently.

ARE MY CONCERNS LEGITIMATE PERFORMANCE ISSUES OR PERSONAL PET PEEVES?

Many times managers say they have an employee with a performance "problem" and they just can't seem to get the employee to fix it. Further investigation often reveals that the manager perceives the situation as an issue, not the employee. Managers often have unclear expectations for employees and/or do not clearly communicate their expectations.

For example, a participant in a training session once said that whenever she leaves the office, she expects her assistant to "handle things." This manager was frustrated because she often returns to the office to find unanswered phone messages. When she was asked if she had explained to her assistant that she expected all phone messages to be returned when she was away, the manager responded meekly, "Well, no, not exactly." The manager said she had never thought about her expectations in that much detail. She assumed the employee knew she was expected to return all the phone calls. She assumed the employee knew what she meant by "handle things." This typical manager realized that the performance issue she thought she was facing was really her own personal issue and was created by her own lack of clarity.

THINK ABOUT IT:

Describe the last time an employee did not perform up to your expectations. What was the issue? Why was it an issue for you and/or the organization? What could you have done to avoid the outcome?

We often know there is an issue, but rarely do we take the time to identify why it is a concern and how that issue affects the organization. Taking the time to ask yourself if the issue is about you or the employee's performance will provide you with the confidence to discuss the issue with the employee because you will be clear about the need to do so.

> Everything that irritates us about others can lead us to an understanding of ourselves.
>
> —Carl Jung

Here are a few questions to ask yourself before you address an employee with a performance issue:

1. *What behavior is not meeting your standards?* You should be able to answer this question in behavioral terms. If it is an "attitude"

or a feeling you have, stop right there. You must be able to give specific, behavioral examples so the employee knows clearly what he or she should stop or start doing. Being "unmotivated" is not specific. Turning in work after an agreed-upon deadline is specific.

Attitudes are what the people think. Attitudes are internal. Attitudes cannot be seen. **Behaviors** are what people do or do not do. Behaviors are observable—you can see them. Behavior can be documented and attitudes cannot.

For example, an employee may have a bad attitude about customer service, but when you discuss the issue with the employee, you will want to discuss the behaviors that indicate poor customer service. You may mention that the employee is slow to return phone calls, did not promptly acknowledge a customer at the front desk, or provided wrong information to a customer.

When addressing performance-related issues in the workplace, it is critical that you focus on behaviors. When you focus on attitudes, the employee is likely to argue with you, since the attitude is not as tangible as the behavior.

2. *What behavior do you want the employee to use more or use less?* If the employee is not doing something in the manner you expect, what do you prefer be done instead? If you can't state your expectations clearly, in behavioral terms, how can you expect the employee to be able to meet those expectations? "Paying more attention to detail" may be your expectation, but it is clearer to share your expectation with a statement such as, "I expect that there will be no grammatical or typographical errors in the report."

3. *How will addressing the issue and changing the behavior improve productivity, safety, confidentiality, or adherence to policy?* If there is not a compelling reason for employees to change their ways, why should they change? We all need to know the "why" behind any change that affects us. If you can't give a reason why employees should behave differently, then you probably should not bring up the issue. The reason for change should be linked to the organization's needs rather than your own needs. For example, the employee with poor customer service behaviors affects the organization by driving away highly valued customers.

Consider this real-life case study as an example of the need to identify specific, business-related behaviors when discussing performance with an employee.

IMPORTANT TERM:

Behavior—The actions or reactions of a person in response to external or internal stimuli. Behaviors are observable things people say, do, or do not say or do.

IMPORTANT TERM:

Attitude—An individual's perspective, thought, or belief about an issue, situation, or person. Attitudes are thoughts and/or feelings that underlie a person's actions.

 HOT TIP!

Differentiate between *attitudes* and *behaviors,* and focus your discussions on behaviors.

CASE STUDY #7
SUSAN AND THE SEASONED ENGINEER

Susan is a dedicated engineering manager. She arrives to work early each day, often works through lunch and sometimes takes work home with her. She has high expectations for herself and for those around her. Susan's lead engineer, Elyse, is effective and responsive in her role as a technical resource for the team. She carries out her duties with competence and with skill. Susan has rarely had to ask Elyse to rework projects. Overall, Susan is pleased with the quality of Elyse's work and with Elyse's ability to anticipate problems and find solutions.

However, Susan has noticed that Elyse does not seem to have the same level of drive that she does. In fact, Susan gets particularly irritated when she sees Elyse drive into the parking lot between 7:45 and 7:55 each morning and then sit in her car to wait until it is almost 8:00 to enter the building. Elyse always makes it to her desk and is ready to work by 8:00 on the nose. However, Susan is irritated that Elyse does not come right into the building when she arrives to get a jump start on the day.

Susan is considering discussing her concerns about promptness, drive, and enthusiasm with Elyse.

- Is Susan's concern about Elyse's behavior a legitimate performance issue or a personal pet peeve?

- What are the potential consequences if Susan addresses this issue with Elyse?

- What would you recommend to Susan about this situation?

When addressing a performance issue with an employee, the issue must be clearly defined and relevant to the job. In other words, it should not be your own pet peeve. In the previous case, Susan clearly has a pet peeve and Elyse's behavior is not job related. Since Elyse is on the job at the expected time and is effective in all her other duties, Susan would be wise to let this issue go. If she brings the issue up with Elyse, she would be hard pressed to justify the relevance of the behavior to Elyse's job performance. Before discussing the issue with the employee, make sure you have considered the impact your discussion will have on the employee and on his or her overall performance and relationship with teammates.

HOW CAN I TELL THE DIFFERENCE BETWEEN BEHAVIORS AND ATTITUDES?

HOT TIP!

Only discuss specific, observable behavioral examples of performance with employees.

Many supervisors get stuck in performance-related discussions when they focus on an employee's attitudes rather than behaviors. Attitudes are the thoughts or feelings that underlie what the employee does on the job. Behaviors are the observable actions an employee takes when on the job. Effective supervisors discuss employee performance in behavioral terms, rather than mentioning attitudes. Here are examples of various behaviors and attitudes:

Attitudes	Behaviors
Enthusiastic	Completing work ahead of schedule
Neglectful	Violating a company policy
Laziness	Arriving to meetings 30 minutes late
Attention to detail	Submitting expense reports without errors or omissions
Difficult to get along with	Shouting loudly at a coworker in the office
Initiative	Completing a service order request before the expected deadline
Service-oriented	Answering the phone within three rings every time
Messy and/or slovenly	Has trouble locating files promptly

THINK ABOUT IT:

Think of a time when you needed to have a conversation with an employee who did not meet your performance expectations. Did you focus on behaviors or attitudes? What was the outcome?

Often supervisors have a conversation with an employee without preparing for the discussion. When this happens, the conversation often becomes a "blame game" or loses focus. By preparing ahead of the discussion and focusing on behaviors, you can ensure that the conversation will stay productive.

HOT TIP!

Prepare a plan that includes specific behavioral examples illustrating the issues that concern you.

WHAT IS THE BEST WAY TO PREPARE FOR A PERFORMANCE-RELATED DISCUSSION?

Once you've decided that an issue is worth discussing with an employee, you must have a plan for the discussion. Otherwise, the discussion will go the direction that you've planned: nowhere.

Sometimes, sitting down with an employee to talk about a performance issue can be intimidating. If you don't have a clear picture of where you want the conversation to end, it will often end with the employee shifting the blame, turning the tables, or otherwise sidetracking you.

A plan for conducting a performance-related discussion with an employee might consist of a list of questions you plan to ask the employee during the conversation. The plan should also include your opening statement and a plan for how you will describe the employee's behavior in specific terms.

To direct the conversation and to ensure that it ends in a productive manner, consider using the following steps as you develop your plan.

Format for an Effective Performance-Related Discussion

Explain the situation and why the issue is important.

- State the facts.
- Explain the impact of the situation on the organization.
- Be concise!

Ask the employee his or her view of the issue.

- Seek information by asking open-ended questions that require employee input or response.
- Summarize the important points as you go.

With the employee, agree on what needs to be accomplished.

- Ask the employee what he or she feels needs to happen or what needs to change.
- Avoid forcing a solution on the employee.
- Be specific about your agreement.

Discuss alternatives for achieving success.

- Ask the employee for ideas to resolve the issue.
- Encourage the employee to suggest a solution he or she could support.
- Weigh the pros and cons of each alternative.

<u>Seek agreement on specific action(s) to be taken by you and the employee.</u>

- Specify who, what, and when.
- Clarify your agreement by asking the employee what he or she will be doing.
- Restate your commitments to the employee.

<u>Express confidence in the employee's ability to resolve the issue and set a follow-up date.</u>

- Be specific about your confidence.
- Be sincere.

> *Don't open up a can of worms without knowing how to get the worms back inside.*
>
> —Mortimer B. Zuckerman

Here's an example of how this conversation might go:

Performance-Related Discussion Example

(in the manager's office or an otherwise private place without distractions)

<u>Explain the situation and why the issue is important.</u>

Manager: Hi, Adele. I've noticed that you've arrived late to two meetings this week. You were fifteen minutes late on Tuesday for the staff meeting, and then you arrived twenty minutes late today for the marketing update. And, when you are late, the team can't proceed without your input. What's going on?

<u>Ask the employee his/her view of the issue.</u>

Adele: I didn't think it was a big deal. On Tuesday the bus was running late and today my alarm didn't go off. You know, I'm not the only one who drags in here late some days. I've noticed that Jane is usually five or ten minutes late, and no one has said anything to her.

Manager: We're talking about your attendance at meetings now, and I want to make sure that we agree on the facts. Do we agree that you were late twice to meetings this week?

Adele: Well, yes, but it really wasn't my fault. The bus has really been a problem lately and the kids. . . . Oh, I'll make sure I'm on time from now on.

<u>With the employee, agree on what needs to be accomplished.</u>

Manager: Okay, then we agree that being on time is important and that your full attendance and participation in meetings is critical?

Adele: Sure.

<u>Discuss alternatives for achieving success.</u>

Manager: Good. Then let's talk about how we're going to make sure that you get to the meetings on time. What ideas do you have to make sure the problems you've had this week don't reoccur?

Adele: I don't know. I'll just make sure I get here on time. I'll be careful to set my alarm each night. Sometimes it doesn't work but I think that's because I don't set it correctly. I also need to just get off the phone or log off the computer when it's time for the meeting to start. Sometimes I lose track of time when I'm at my desk.

Manager: That's a good idea. Are there any issues you think I can help you with so that you are on time for future meetings?

Adele: There's nothing you can do. I know I need to have a back-up if the bus is running late or if I miss it. I know my sister sometimes has friends who drive her to work when she misses the bus.

Manager: That's an important thing to consider. Is there anything else that might be a barrier to getting to your meetings on time?

Adele: Well, I'll be honest. I'm not always excited about attending those marketing updates. They can get pretty boring, and sometimes they don't even relate to my work.

Manager: I understand that sometimes the group focuses on issues that are not directly relevant to your clients and your territory. What do you think we could do to address this challenge?

Adele: I guess I could review the agenda before each meeting and ask Tom, the marketing manager, to list issues that are relevant to my territory first on the agenda. Then, when the conversation turns to other territories or issues that don't relate to me, I could excuse myself.

Manager: Your participation in those meetings is important and if that will work for you and for Tom, then it will work for me.

Seek agreement on specific action(s) to be taken by you and the employee.

Manager: Let's summarize what we've come up with. You are going to make sure that you get here on time for each weekly staff meeting. And, you're going to talk to Tom, the marketing manager, about adjusting his agenda to allow you to be there for the agenda items that only relate to your territory. Is that right?

Adele: Yeah, that sounds okay. I'm really sorry. I'll make sure I'm a little more prompt from now on. I really didn't know it was a big deal.

Express confidence in the employee's ability to resolve the issue and set a follow-up date.

Manager: I'm confident that this is not going to be an issue again. When you put your mind to something, you usually succeed. Let's meet in two weeks to see how things are going. How about meeting on the 21st at 1:30?

Adele: That works for me. Thanks.

> *Great organizations are not made of great people. They are made of great relationships between people.*
>
> —Larry Reynolds

HOW CAN I MAKE SURE THAT PERFORMANCE-RELATED DISCUSSIONS DO NOT GET DERAILED?

Some managers think they know how to solve problems if only their employees would listen. Many managers feel it is their job to provide the answers to every issue raised by employees. However, the best managers know it is the other way around. To gain employee support and buy-in, great managers do more listening than talking. They ask more questions than they offer solutions and they believe others have good ideas to offer.

> Rather weigh the will of the speaker than the worth of the words.
>
> —English proverb

THINK ABOUT IT:

In the conversation with the employee you described previously who did not meet your expectations, how could you have improved the outcome of the discussion? What steps in the discussion format did you overlook? What was the impact of leaving these steps out?

Usually, if a performance-related conversation turns bad, it's likely that the supervisor has not planned well and has not followed the essential six steps. By not listening to the employee's perspective on the issue, or by not gaining the employee's agreement that there is an issue, you may be setting yourself up for a derailed conversation. Gaining employee support and buy-in ensures success in performance-related discussions.

HOW CAN I IMPROVE MY LISTENING SKILLS?

Here are several ideas to help you be a better listener in these challenging conversations.

1. *Ask questions that show you care.* Rather than telling employees there is an issue that needs to be addressed, try asking them what they think the issue is, based on the symptoms. Then, when you listen, they will be more likely to offer solutions they can endorse. Effective question asking is the key to open communication.

> Feedback without compassion is judgment.
>
> —Anonymous

2. *Ask questions that elicit buy-in.*   The next time someone comes to you for advice, resist the temptation to give them the answer. This is tough for many who have "been there, done that." However, if you really want employees to believe in the solution, ask them what they think the best solution would be. Through effective questioning, great managers lead people to the best solutions.

HOT TIP!

Listen more than you speak.

3. *Zip it!*   One of the hardest things for motivated, high achievers to do is to *not* offer their own opinion. However, this is one skill that can help you build relationships faster than anything else. After you ask a question of your staff, close your mouth, maintain eye contact, and wait for a response. Resist the tendency to give your own answer. A little bit of silence may be difficult, but it won't kill you.

4. *Paraphrase what you hear them say.*   Once you get a response from employees, try restating what they've said. They are guaranteed to know you are listening when you paraphrase their words. Try using phrases like, "I think I'm hearing you say . . . " or "Do you mean . . . ?" or "Are you saying . . . ?" Then, go back to step three and zip it!

> *Be swift to hear, slow to speak, slow to wrath.*
>
> —James 1:19

Being a great manager means being a great listener. You may have great ideas and skills yourself, but as a manager, your job is to cultivate the great ideas and skills of others. In fact, Max De Pree said, "In some South Pacific cultures, a speaker holds a conch shell as a symbol of a temporary position of authority. Leaders must understand who holds the conch—that is, who should be listened to and when." Let employees hold the conch shell when discussing performance-related issues and they will find their own solutions.

Performance Checklist

1. Differentiate between true performance issues and your own personal pet peeves before talking with an employee about his or her performance.

2. Ensure that you are not going to create more problems by raising the issue and strive to make sure that what you say is perceived as fair.

3. Be careful to distinguish between behaviors and attitudes and to focus on behaviors in performance-related discussions.

4. Create and follow a plan for conducting performance-related discussions and keep the plan focused on getting a commitment to achieve job-related, measurable results.

5. In a performance-related discussion, ask more questions than you answer. Remember to listen!

What Did You Learn?

TRUE OR FALSE QUESTIONS
Circle T or F to indicate whether each of the following statements is true or false.

T   F   1. A pet peeve is something the employee does that is directly related to the job and job performance.

T   F   2. It is important for the supervisor to plan the performance-related discussion before talking with the employee about the issue.

T   F   3. The first step in a performance-related discussion should be to explain the situation to the employee and to highlight why the issue is important to you and the organization.

T   F   4. It is more important for a manager to talk in a performance-related discussion than to listen.

MULTIPLE CHOICE QUESTIONS
Circle the letter next to the best answer for each question.

1. Of the following issues, which is an example of a *specific* behavior?
   (a) Being unmotivated
   (b) Having a bad attitude
   (c) Arriving to work fifteen minutes late
   (d) Having no tact

2. The performance-related discussion should include all of the following steps except:
   (a) Asking the employee for his or her view of the issue
   (b) Expressing confidence in the employee
   (c) Discussing alternatives
   (d) Telling the employee what he or she must do

3. An effective practice when conducting performance-related discussions is to:

   (a) Explain a laundry list of problems the employee is encountering

   (b) Ask a lot of questions and listen to the employee's response

   (c) Tell the employee that he or she has no choice in how the problem is resolved

   (d) None of the above

4. Which of the following statements about performance-related discussions is *not* true?

   (a) Managers should paraphrase what they hear before reacting to what the employee has to say.

   (b) Managers should plan ahead to avoid a derailed conversation.

   (c) Employees should be asked for their input on how to address performance issues.

   (d) All of the above are true.

OBJECTIVE QUESTIONS

1. What tools and steps can a manager use to conduct effective performance-related discussions?

2. Why is it more important to focus on an employee's behavior during a performance-related discussion rather than on attitudes?

Rating Performance Objectively and Legally

Just definitions either prevent or put an end to a dispute.

—Nathaniel Emmons

This chapter will enable you to:

- Justify and apply the ratings that appear on performance evaluation forms.
- Differentiate performance using various rating categories.
- Lead employees to understand differences in performance as defined in each rating category.
- Understand the ways you can make your performance rating choices legally defensible.

Most performance management systems require factors of performance to be rated and an overall rating to be assigned to the employee's performance. In some organizations, this rating is based on a calculation. In other organizations, the supervisor is expected to make a judgment on the overall rating, often based on the cumulative nature of the individual ratings listed in the report. However the overall rating is determined, it must reflect the clear expectations for performance that were established at the beginning of the rating period, and it should send a clear message to employees about the sum total of their performance.

IS THERE ONE BEST RATING SCALE FOR A PERFORMANCE EVALUATION SYSTEM?

The Society for Human Resource Management recommends that organizations implement a four-point scale for rating performance. With a four-level scale there is no middle of the road rating that serves as the default. For example, with a three- or five-level scale (A-**B**-C or A-B-**C**-D-E rating choices), the middle rating can serve as the "average." In a four-level scale managers are forced to make a choice between ratings at either the lower or higher end of the scale. For this reason, a four level scale is preferred.

Whether your organization chooses to use a three, four, five, or other rating scale, the number of rating choices is not as relevant as how they are defined. For ratings to be justified, it's helpful to have a clear definition of what each rating level means. Whether your organization has adopted a scale of three, four, five, or ten, if the levels are not defined, both employees and managers will be challenged to apply them.

HOW DO I EXPLAIN THE RATING CATEGORIES TO EMPLOYEES?

Before you assign a rating to an employee's performance, ask yourself: "What will it take to get the highest rating?" Your employees may also ask you this question.

If your answer is, "It's not possible to get the highest rating," then you've taken the easy way out. It should be possible to achieve any of the rating levels listed on the evaluation form. However, it is up to you to explain to the employee what level of performance is required to achieve the highest levels. Do not cop out with an answer like, "You have to walk on water." This has no meaning to the employee. Be specific and be clear about job behaviors and outcomes that the employee must display to earn each rating listed on the scale. You should have examples for the complete range of possible ratings.

Consider this case study as an example of why it is important to clearly define the performance required to earn each rating on the performance evaluation form.

CASE STUDY #8
THE NEW, ENTHUSIASTIC ASSOCIATE

Lorraine has considered herself an excellent supervisor for years and has never had a problem explaining and defending the ratings she gives to employees on their annual performance evaluations.

She has worked hard to include specific examples of performance to justify each rating. She also continuously communicates with employees about their progress so that there are no surprises at the end of the rating period.

Lorraine recently hired a new associate who is full of energy and enthusiasm. Wayne is inquisitive, hard-working, and dedicated to learning everything he can about his new job and his new employer. In fact, Wayne asks more questions than any employee Lorraine has ever supervised.

Within the first week of Wayne's employment, Lorraine and Wayne sit down to discuss his performance goals and Lorraine's expectations. While explaining the organization's performance management system, Lorraine is surprised by a question from Wayne that she feels is particularly challenging. Wayne asks, "What will it take for me to get the highest rating in each of the categories on the form?" Wayne is a high achiever and has told Lorraine several times that he does not like to "fail." Lorraine is not sure how to respond to this tough question.

- How should Lorraine respond to Wayne's tough question?

- If Wayne does not receive the highest rating in every category on the form, does this mean that he has "failed" on the job? How would you explain your rationale to Wayne?

- What steps would you recommend to Lorraine in addressing Wayne's question?

HOT TIP!
Don't attempt to rate an employee's performance until you can clearly describe the level of performance associated with each category.

THINK ABOUT IT:

What will it take for an employee you supervise to earn the highest overall rating possible on your organization's performance evaluation form? Describe the actions and behaviors that you would expect this employee to exhibit. Be specific.

IMPORTANT TERM:

Rating period—The period of time for which an employee will be evaluated using a performance evaluation system. Rating periods can be one quarter, one year, or any other time period the organization establishes.

If your organization provides you with a definition of each rating category, that is helpful. If the organization does not, you should develop your own definitions for each level and share those definitions with the employee at the beginning of the rating period. The definitions should be established by the organization's leaders and should represent the collective agreement of the leadership team. If your organization does not provide such guidance, don't wait for someone else to do this for you! You can still make your expectations clear by defining the rating levels yourself with the staff's input.

Whatever method is used to establish the definitions of the rating scale, the definitions should be used to differentiate varying levels of performance. The more specific the descriptors are, the easier it is to explain to employees why they were rated the way they were.

WHAT SHOULD RATING DEFINITIONS LOOK LIKE?

If your organization does not provide a clearly written definition to differentiate the rating categories, the following examples might be helpful to you. You'll notice that the terms used to describe each rating level may vary.

Sample #1 Five-Level Rating Scale

Consistently Exceeds Expectations—This rating is for exceptional performance over the entire rating period. This rating is rare and is usually reserved for those employees who excel in every area of the job or for those who successfully complete an unusually demanding special project during the rating period, in addition to regular duties.

Often Exceeds Expectations—This rating means the employee is perceived as highly competent and does more than just meet the job requirements. An overall rating of *Often Exceeds Expectations* should be perceived as a strong endorsement of the employee's work.

Meets Expectations—This rating should be interpreted as a "job well done." It is appropriate for employees who meet the standards for the position and are doing an effective job.

Often Does Not Meet Expectations—This rating means performance is unacceptable often enough that significant improvement is required. The major purpose of an overall rating of *Often Does Not Meet Expectations* is to focus the employee's attention on the areas that need improvement and to assist the employee in setting reasonable and attainable goals. Performance at this level is expected to improve, and the preparation of a performance improvement plan is recommended. An employee who cannot or will not improve overall performance will face probation, demotion, or possible termination.

Consistently Does Not Meet Expectations—This rating means that continued performance at this level will not be tolerated and immediate improvement is required. A performance improvement plan should be required for overall ratings of *Consistently Does Not Meet Expectations*. An employee who continues to perform at this level should be terminated.

Sample #2 Four-Level Rating Scale

Far Exceeds Standards—The level of performance demonstrated is consistently and significantly above acceptable and established standards. Achieves performance objectives at a superior level and demonstrates exceptional skill levels.

Exceeds Standards—Performance is consistently above the acceptable standard demonstrating high skill levels. Achieves performance objectives in an excellent manner.

Effective—Performance is consistently appropriate, demonstrating acceptable skill levels. Achieves performance objectives.

Development Strategy Required—Performance is less than acceptable and needs improvement. Direction, supervision, and learning are required if performance objectives are to be achieved. The employee needs to make performance improvements within a specified time period.

Sample #3 Three-Level Rating Scale

Outstanding—Performance exceeds all expectations; volume of work produced continually exceeds expectations; superior quality of work; rework is rarely required; exceptional customer service as may be evidenced by commendations; all objectives and tasks achieved before the deadline; tasks completed with little or no supervision; demonstrates high level of initiative; accepts and helps to implement change; mentors others in the workplace.

Successful—Performance meets and often exceeds expectations; produces expected volume of work; high quality of work; little rework required; excellent customer service provided without preventable complaints; all objectives and job tasks achieved on or before the deadline; tasks completed with minimal supervision; responds appropriately when directed and often shows initiative; accepts changes being implemented; contributes to the team's mission and goals.

Does Not Meet Expectations—Performance is less than acceptable; does not produce expected volume of work; quality of work does not meet expectations; customer service skills need improvement and do not meet the expectation of our culture; some or all objectives or tasks not met by the deadline and without valid justification; tasks completed with the need for continual supervision; demonstrates little initiative; resists changes; creates friction and conflict on the team.

You'll notice that the labels used to describe each level are different in each of the examples. This is because the words chosen to describe varying levels of performance are not as important as the actual definitions and how they are understood by the people who will use them.

THINK ABOUT IT:

How do you define the rating levels in your organization's performance management system? If definitions are provided by your organization, are they clear enough to explain performance expectations for employees? Why or why not?

HOW CAN I HELP EMPLOYEES BETTER UNDERSTAND THE DIFFERENCES IN EACH RATING CATEGORY?

It is good to have these definitions and share them with employees as a way to explain your expectations. It is GREAT if the employees can participate in the development of the definitions because it leads to greater buy-in and understanding about what it takes to earn each level of performance rating.

> Motivation is everything. You can do the work of two people, but you can't be two people. Instead, you have to inspire the next guy down the line and get him to inspire his people.
>
> —Lee Iacocca

Here's an exercise you can try at a staff meeting that will foster discussion about performance ratings and help employees better understand each rating level.

Staff Meeting Exercise

Ask the staff to describe specific things an employee would need to do (behaviors) that would earn him or her each of the ratings for the performance dimension on the rating form. Give staff members a piece flipchart paper or newsprint on which to list the rating levels. Under each rating level, ask them to define what an employee would need to do to earn each rating. The flipchart for the definition of ratings for "overall performance" might look something like this:

Overall Performance

Consistently Exceeds Expectations:

Often Exceeds Expectations:

Meets Expectations:

Does Not Meet Expectations:

This exercise can be applied to a discussion about overall rating, or it can be used when defining individual performance dimensions (job skills, work relationships, communication, initiative, etc.) that may also be rated on the form.

The result of a discussion about overall performance might look something like this:

Consistently Exceeds Expectations—Broadly influences others in a positive manner; even in stressful situations, demonstrates a positive approach to change and maximizes the opportunities created by change; fosters teamwork and positive relationships with everyone they come in contact with; written materials are error free; communication is concise and accurate; is used as a resource in communicating material to others.

HOT TIP!

Ask your team members to help you define the behaviors associated with each rating category.

Often Exceeds Expectations—Goes out of the way to cooperate and get along with others; works to develop rapport with others so that conflict can be resolved; expresses disagreement by offering productive alternatives; adjusts quickly to new priorities and helps foster acceptance in the workplace; uses oral and written communication skills to foster positive working relationships; written material and/or oral presentations seldom contain errors; clear and easily understood.

Meets Expectations—Recognizes that change is part of the job and attempts to help foster changes in the workplace; expresses disagreement in a respectful manner; does not participate in conflict situations without attempting to resolve the differences; clearly expresses ideas verbally and in writing; cooperative; gets along well with others; any errors in communication do not hinder the recipient's understanding of the message.

Does Not Meet Expectations—Always inflexible to changing circumstances; demonstrates negativity toward work group members or toward company goals; initiates conflict without the desire to resolve differences; written material and/or oral presentations are confusing and difficult to follow or understand; fails to record or recite pertinent information; frequently complains; not a team player.

HOW CAN I ENSURE THAT MY RATINGS ARE DEFENSIBLE IF THEY ARE EVER CHALLENGED?

In rare occasions an employee may choose to dispute or challenge a performance rating. In most organizations, such ratings are not part of the formal appeal process, and employees are encouraged to express their views about the rating in the comments section or on an attachment to the evaluation. Some organizations have an appeal process in place for addressing disagreements about performance ratings. Whatever process your organization uses, remembering two things will keep you out of hot water when rating performance:

1. The focus of the evaluation must be **job-related.**
2. The more **specific facts** you include in the evaluation, the easier it will be to justify the ratings.

If you include only job-related, specific examples of performance, your ratings will be justifiable and substantiated. If you are vague and judgmental in your assessment, you are opening yourself up to a challenge.

THINK ABOUT IT:

Look at the past performance evaluations you have prepared. Did you focus on job-related, specific facts? Did you mention things that were not specific or clearly defined?

At a minimum, it is critical that you define what each rating level means for the jobs you supervise. The human resources department and/or executive team can provide you with general or standardized definitions, but only you, the immediate supervisor, and the employee can determine how the general definitions apply to the job in question.

Performance Checklist

1. Clearly define what each rating level means for each performance factor and for overall performance.

2. The number of rating levels or categories is not as important as how clearly they are defined between you and the employee.

3. Involving employees in a discussion about each rating level will help to clarify performance expectations and how ratings will be applied.

4. Focus on job-related, specific examples of performance to fairly and legally justify performance ratings.

What Did You Learn?

TRUE OR FALSE QUESTIONS
Circle T or F to indicate whether each of the following statements is true or false.

T   F   1. In most performance evaluation systems, rating categories are used to describe an employee's performance.

T   F   2. It should not be possible for employees to earn the highest rating in your organization's performance evaluation system.

T   F   3. Employees will be less likely to disagree with a performance rating if a clear definition of the rating is provided.

T   F   4. It is the responsibility of the human resources department to define how factors on the performance evaluation form apply to each job.

MULTIPLE CHOICE QUESTIONS
Circle the letter next to the best answer for each question.

1. Which of the following is not a logical definition of an overall performance rating of *Does Not Meet Expectations?*

   (a) Written materials do not make sense and contain errors

   (b) Received multiple complaints from customers

   (c) Adjusts quickly to new priorities

   (d) Frequently complains

2. Which of the following is a logical definition of an overall performance rating of *Meets Expectations?*

   (a) Quality of work always exceeds what is expected

   (b) Produces expected volume of work

   (c) Misses deadlines and due dates

   (d) Consistently receives recognition for professional accomplishments

3. Employees can best understand the rating levels on the performance evaluation form if they:

   (a) Read the manual on performance evaluations

   (b) Hear their supervisor explain the definitions

   (c) Figure it out on their own

   (d) Participate in a facilitated discussion to define each rating level

4. To ensure that you can justify the ratings you assign to an employee's performance, it is critical that the evaluation is:

   (a) Job related

   (b) Specific

   (c) a and b

   (d) None of the above

OBJECTIVE QUESTIONS

1. What is the value of working with employees to define how they feel each rating level applies to the job? What concerns do you have about this exercise?

2. In addition to a staff discussion, how can you ensure that your employees clearly understand how the rating levels on the performance evaluation form apply to their job so that there are no surprises at evaluation time?

Writing the Performance Evaluation Document

Aim for success, not perfection. Never give up your right to be wrong, because then you will lose the ability to learn new things and move forward with your life.

—Dr. David M. Burns

This chapter will enable you to:

- Integrate your documentation effectively into the written performance evaluation.
- Solicit and use the employee's self-evaluation.
- Phrase the performance evaluation document so that it is specific and action oriented.
- Describe poor performance in a productive and encouraging way.
- Write effective and defensible evaluations.

Writing the performance evaluation document is a task that many supervisors procrastinate. Some supervisors use these excuses:

- "I don't know where to start."

- "I'm not a good writer."

- "I'm afraid the employee won't like what I write."

- "I work best when I write it at the last minute."

- "I'll take the easy way out and just let employees write their own evaluation and I'll sign it."

All the excuses in the world don't change the fact that writing the performance evaluation is the supervisor's responsibility, and it should include an adequate amount of facts about the employee's performance that reflect the entire rating period.

HOT TIP!

Preparing a well-documented performance evaluation is a primary responsibility of the supervisor.

WHAT IS THE SOURCE OF INFORMATION TO BE INCLUDED IN THE PERFORMANCE EVALUATION?

Supervisors often complain that they don't know where to start. The best place to start is to review the collected data.

The performance evaluation should be based on factual data, collected from a variety of sources. You should not base the evaluation solely on your own observations or beliefs. Use the data available to you from a variety of sources to form an unbiased and fair evaluation of employees' performance. If you do so, employees are likely to feel that you have fairly evaluated their performance, rather than just randomly passing judgment on them. Let's face it. Performance evaluations are inherently subjective. The data is a way to add objectivity to your assessment.

The following data sources may be used to gain information about an employee's performance:

- Goals and expectations upon which you and the employee agreed upon

- Customer feedback

- Coworker feedback

- Feedback from other supervisors who may work with the employee

- Strategic business plans (visions, missions, organizational goals, etc.)

- Activity/progress reports and/or memos or e-mails related to the employee's performance

- Notes made in your supervisor's file

- Commendations and recognition received from others

- Disciplinary actions filed throughout the rating period

- Quantitative performance records used to track the employee's output

- Changes that have affected the employee's performance, including reorganizations, staffing, budget, market developments, etc.

HOT TIP!

Use a customer survey to solicit additional feedback from customers about each employee's performance.

THINK ABOUT IT:

What are the best sources of input you can use in evaluating your employee's work performance?

None of these sources of performance information should be used alone. The evaluation should be based on a compilation of the data collected. You must balance the data received from a variety of sources to ensure that the final evaluation reflects all perspectives. Once the data is collected, you can use it to tell the story about the employee's performance rather than worrying about "what to write."

> When you're off on a business trip or vacation, pretend you're a customer. Telephone some part of your organization and ask for help.
>
> —Robert Townsend

Don't be overwhelmed with the amount of data you may have collected. Instead, look for:

- Data that supports trends

- Significant events that were meaningful

- Factual, firsthand knowledge rather than assumptions or rumors

WHAT ABOUT THE EMPLOYEE'S SELF-EVALUATION?

It is helpful to get the employee's input before you begin writing the evaluation document. Ask the employee to provide you with any information he or she has that will help you to evaluate his or her performance. The purpose of this request is to make sure you have all the data available to prepare a fair and objective evaluation. Remind the employee that while you have kept records about his or her performance, you may have missed something along the way.

You might ask for things like:

■ A list of significant accomplishments

■ Improvements the employee recommended and/or implemented

■ Letters or e-mails of commendation the employee received that have not been forwarded to you

■ Training completed that you may have not recorded

■ Anything else the employee feels is important to share that will give you a complete look at his or her performance

DO NOT ask the employee to fill out the evaluation form on his or her own and submit it to you. This approach leads to the employee feeling as if the evaluation duties are being delegated. Employees want your opinion and feedback, however you convey it. Those supervisors who ask their employees to complete their own evaluations and who do not add significantly to the content of the employees' evaluations are seen as lazy, as cowards, or as both.

Instead, try using a standard format for soliciting feedback from employees about their work performance. The following example could be used to ask employees for their input and ideas:

Employee Self-Evaluation Format

This is to confirm our meeting on _____ to discuss your performance over the last _____ months/year and to create a plan for your performance for the coming year.

Your input is essential to the success of our meeting and I value your ideas. Please respond to the following questions in as much detail as possible. I will use this information as I prepare the performance evaluation documents.

Please return this sheet to me by _____ so that I can incorporate your perspectives into the evaluation.

1. What do you consider to be your most significant accomplishments since our last performance discussion?

2. What were your greatest challenges since our last performance discussion?

3. What new challenges or goals would you like to pursue in the upcoming rating period?

4. What can the organization or I do to help you improve your performance over the next rating period?

5. Please tell me about anything else I need to consider in preparing your performance evaluation.

The use of an employee self-evaluation should be seen as an optional exercise. While it is recommended that supervisors ask for input to ensure that performance events and details are not overlooked, if employees choose not to provide input to the process, they should not be required to do so.

> The wise manager uses the subordinate's self-appraisal as only one suggestion in a whole mine of performance information.
>
> —Dick Grote

THINK ABOUT IT:

How can you best solicit performance feedback and input from your employees? How are they likely to react to your request for input?

IMPORTANT TERM

Rating form—Also referred to as the performance evaluation document, the organization-specific form that a supervisor uses to complete a performance evaluation.

HOW CAN I MAKE SURE I WRITE A CLEAR AND EFFECTIVE PERFORMANCE EVALUATION DOCUMENT?

Before you put pen to paper or fingers to keyboard, be sure you can answer the following questions. This checklist will help you to more clearly communicate your message in the performance evaluation.

Pre-Performance Evaluation Checklist

Before you write an evaluation or talk with an employee about his or her performance evaluation, ask yourself these key preparation questions:

- ☑ What background information and facts exist that relate to the performance?
- ☑ What specific behaviors will you encourage the employee continue to use?
- ☑ What specific behaviors will you coach the employee to change?
- ☑ What are the consequences if the employee is unwilling to change?
- ☑ What are your immediate objectives for this evaluation?
- ☑ What are your long-range goals related to this employee's performance?
- ☑ How can you better support this employee?
- ☑ Are you in control, confident, and ready to discuss the issues that you intend to present in the evaluation?

WHAT DO EFFECTIVELY WRITTEN PERFORMANCE EVALUATIONS HAVE IN COMMON?

Well-written performance evaluations are full of specific, real-life examples to support the ratings assigned. The real life examples make the evaluation objective rather than subjective. Here are a few tips for creating well-written comments in the performance evaluation document:

- *Refer to predetermined standards and goals.* If you and the employee have established clear expectations for the job, including specific goals, and if these expectations have been written down, the performance evaluation is a summary of whether the employee met or did not meet the expectations. These standards may come from a variety of sources including the job description, organizational goals, quantitative standards, and the clearly defined expectations. Without a baseline against which you can compare the performance, on what else will you base the rating?

- *Cite examples of performance.* If you have kept specific and detailed records of the employee's performance, these can be the basis for comments on the performance evaluation. If you have saved e-mails, letters of commendation, and actual work samples, you can describe these in the performance evaluation, and they serve as sound support for your ratings, whether they are positive, negative, or neutral.

- *Be objective and specific rather than subjective and general.* One of the most common criticisms about performance evaluations is that they are too subjective. The more specific examples and factual evidence that are presented, the more likely the evaluation will be well received. It's easy to argue with opinion, but it's difficult to argue with facts.

- *Write in a conversational tone.* Do you write "about" the employee, or do you write "to" the employee? The ideal tone to use in a performance evaluation is the more personal tone of writing **to** the employee. For example, "Steve, you met four of the six goals that were set for this year" is an example of the comments being conversational in nature. By using the employee's name and by using pronouns like "you" and "your," the written comments take on a softer, friendlier appeal. When the comments are written "about" the employee, as in "Mr. Finley met four of the six goals that were set for him this year," a distance is created between you and the employee. While some supervisors would like to hide behind a more formal tone, it does nothing to develop rapport between you and the employee.

- *Strive for balance in terms of positive and constructive comments.* Solid performance-related comments should be both positive and constructive. Even the very best worker can benefit from a suggestion for improvement or focus for the coming rating period. And even the worst employee has done something right. Make sure both ends of the spectrum are mentioned in the evaluation comments.

> *Never giving criticism without praise is a strict rule for me. No matter what you are criticizing, you must find something good to say—both before and after. . . . Criticize the act, not the person.*
>
> —Mary Kay Ash

THINK ABOUT IT:

What was the best performance evaluation document you ever received and why was it so good? What was the worst performance evaluation document you've ever received and why was it bad?

Strong evaluation documents are specific, balanced, and job-related. By striving to convey a balanced picture of the employee's performance, you can create a document that will be useful and motivating to the employee.

 HOT TIP!

Phrase performance comments using action verbs that make your ideas vivid and clear.

WHAT ARE SOME HELPFUL WORDS TO GET THE PROCESS STARTED?

The comments in the performance evaluation document will be much richer and more vivid if the employee's behavior is described using action verbs. Action verbs add movement and specificity and describe what the employee has done during the rating period. Here are a few action verbs you can use to generate ideas for new ways to describe an employee's performance. Use these words when writing performance evaluations to convey specific, job-related behaviors.

Accentuate	Accept	Amplify
Analyze	Arrange	Adhere
Act	Listen	Respond

Advise	Articulate	Assemble
Build	Circulate	Coach
Collaborate	Complete	Consider
Compare	Coordinate	Develop
Draft	Emphasize	Encourage
Enforce	Exhibit	Facilitate
Generate	Guide	Handle
Improve	Influence	Ensure
Maintain	Meet	Manage
Negotiate	Observe	Operate
Oversee	Participate	Perform
Prepare	Prioritize	Promote
Reinforce	Rely	Resolve
Solve	Stimulate	Submit
Survey	Translate	Use

These words can be used to describe an employee's behavior in specific terms. For example:

- Cory, you are good at complex plumbing assignments.
  IS NOT AS SPECIFIC AS
- Cory, you *solve* complex plumbing problems without assistance.

- Michelle, you are able to serve the highest priority customers.
  IS NOT AS SPECIFIC AS
- Michelle, you *prioritize* your heavy workload and ensure that the highest priority customers get the service they deserve.

- Marla, you were a good leader of the employee recognition team.
  IS NOT AS SPECIFIC AS
- Marla, you *generated* employee participation readily when you effectively facilitated the employee recognition team.

- Megan, your reports are on time each week.
  IS NOT AS SPECIFIC AS
- Megan, you *submit* your purchase orders and other financial reports on time each week, which is appreciated by the Accounting Department.

By using action verbs and by focusing on the specific outcomes of the employee's work, you can create vivid and clearly understandable descriptions in the comments section of the performance evaluation.

HOW CAN POOR PERFORMANCE BE DESCRIBED DIPLOMATICALLY?

Most supervisors find it easy to describe performance when the performance meets or exceeds the expectations. When the performance does not meet expectations, it is harder to be specific and clear. Here is a formula that will help you describe not-so-great performance in a way that is positive and offers an opportunity for improvement to the employee.

Formula for Describing a Performance Improvement Opportunity

"You can (*name something they will value or benefit from*), if you (*name something they need to do differently*)."

Here are a few examples:

For the employee who doesn't give enough attention to details:

- You can improve the accuracy of your monthly statements if you proofread your statements before submitting them.

For the employee who doesn't listen well:

- You can improve your monthly customer ratings if you listen to customers' needs carefully before responding to their requests.

For the employee who wastes time:

- You can complete your daily task list and your annual goals if you concentrate on high payoff activities like returning customer calls and fulfilling orders.

For the employee who is unprepared:

- You can appear more organized and confident at staff meetings if you gather and bring the necessary data, including the sales report, prior to each meeting.

For the employee who is resistant to change:

- You can be seen as a stronger team player if you adopt new instructions, situations, methods, and procedures quickly and without resistance.

By stating the benefit first, you are acknowledging that the employee will profit from changing behavior.

> Develop the winning edge; small differences in your performance can lead to large differences in your results.
>
> —Brian Tracy

Rather than forcing or mandating the change, you are giving the employee an opportunity to save face and correct the behavior without a lot of hoopla or pressure.

THINK ABOUT IT:

What is an example of a performance improvement that you will need to describe in the next performance evaluation you complete? How will you write it as an opportunity for the employee?

HOT TIP!

Think of every performance issue as an opportunity for improvement and growth.

Turning a potentially negative situation into an opportunity for improvement allows you to help the employee improve performance and puts the responsibility for the change in the employee's hands.

WHAT ARE THE DOS AND DON'TS FOR WRITING PERFORMANCE EVALUATION COMMENTS?

Writing comments on the performance evaluation takes thought and effort. This is effort the employee expects to see. Remember the following dos and don'ts and writing comments will be easier.

Do	Don't
Address the employee in the second person (Tom, in the past year you . . .).	Write your comments in the third person (The employee met all the goals . . .).
Use a conversational style and tone.	Use vague generalities (good job, adequate, poor, enough, etc.).

Do	Don't
Be specific about accomplishments by using real-life examples of performance.	Use "flowery" language if it is out of character for you ("You were fabulously eloquent at the banquet when you articulated your ideas about . . . ").
Be tactful about shortcomings by using the formula for describing a performance improvement opportunity.	Make references to medical conditions of any kind.
Express appreciation for the employee's efforts.	Use derogatory terms, including racial, age, gender, national origin, disability, or other topics that could result in a charge of discrimination.
Incorporate comments solicited from the employee and coworkers that are positive and supportive.	Use comments from coworkers that are negative as a way to substantiate lower ratings without other data to support them.
Mention special awards and recognition.	Compare the employee to other employees ("You should be more like Julie").
Quantify your remarks when appropriate ("You have increased your output by 25 percent").	Bring up concerns or issues that have never been mentioned to the employee previously.
Focus on past performance.	Predict future performance ("I'm sure your performance will continue at an outstanding level next year").

Consider this case study as an example of how vague and/or unclear comments on the performance evaluation can backfire.

CASE STUDY #9
HOW CAN I SAY THIS?

George has just finished drafting the comments section of Carol's performance evaluation. As usual, George was in a hurry to meet the deadline for the evaluation.

Carol has been an effective customer service representative in terms of the number of customers she has served. However, Carol has received numerous complaints from customers related to her accuracy and tactfulness.

Here are the comments that George hastily prepared on the performance evaluation form: "Carol served her customers effectively this year by responding to calls and following up on requests. She was not the top performer in the department but her performance met expectations. Overall, Carol can improve by making sure she meets her customers' needs. Carol has potential to be a great rep if she wants to be."

- What concerns do you have about the comments that George has prepared?

- What are the likely results if George submits these comments to Carol on her performance evaluation?

- Rewrite the comments on Carol's performance evaluation so that they are more specific and constructive. Make up details, if necessary, to make the comments specific.

WHAT DO GOOD PERFORMANCE EVALUATION COMMENTS LOOK LIKE?

Sometimes it helps to have examples when you are preparing an especially difficult performance evaluation. In this section you'll find examples of particularly effective comments made by supervisors on performance evaluation documents and a discussion of why each is effective.

> Judy, you are a very willing and conscientious employee who never hesitates to "go the extra mile." You accept new projects and responsibilities with undying eagerness and complete your given tasks in a timely fashion. This is evidenced by your positive CAN-DO attitude with the Cow project. Your effort and involvement with this project has helped our customers by substantially minimizing the conflicts customers face and by eliminating the inconvenience to vendors. I received a letter of appreciation from the Executive Director's secretary commending you for handling a special request. I appreciate your coordination efforts during the annual Festival of the Farms. The event gets bigger and better each year as a result of your hard work.

These comments are effective because:

- They are written in a conversational tone.

> *Truth does not change according to our ability to stomach it.*
> —Flannery O'Connor

- Specific examples are included (Gow project, Festival of the Farms).

- Additional outside sources were used to substantiate the evaluation.

Larry, you successfully accomplished the goals of assisting with the procedure revision, screening of applications, processing new requests, and responding to work orders within a two-day period. Due to the advanced level and nature of these goals, I want to emphasize the importance of your accomplishments in these particular areas. I commend you for a job well done. In particular, I was impressed by your handling of the Green case, which required you to go to the citizen's home to resolve their complaint. This is an example of your going above and beyond the call of duty.

There have been problems with the GGG form. You missed the deadline for reformatting the GGG form and did not communicate that you were having a problem completing the assignment. As a result, the Accounts Division was unable to process the July invoices. This can be avoided in the future by letting me know when problems come up that may delay the project.

These comments are effective because:

- They list specific goals that were accomplished.

- They cite specific examples of performance (the Green case).

- Areas for improvement are acknowledged, giving the employee an area for development in the future.

Brian, the nature of our business requires constant, positive interactions with coworkers to effectively support the organization's goals. You have interjected negative comments about the organization and its policies into conversations with others. For example, on 8/9/XX, you argued with James at the staff meeting about the payroll cutoff date. The conversation was negative in tone and interfered with the entire staff's ability to focus on the task at hand.

When this occurs, especially in your interactions with new staff members, it has proven to be highly disruptive. Increased effort on your part, along with the willingness you have shown to improve the technical aspects of your job, can successfully be transferred to improving your interactions with coworkers.

These comments are effective because:

- They give specific examples of behavior that was unacceptable.

- They tie the need for improved performance into a business need.

- They focus on the future and the expectation for improved performance.

Gary, you continue to work independently, demonstrating a strong understanding of the tax code. You always strive to stay current and apply the code in a consistent manner to all with whom you come in contact. Your willingness to share both your audit techniques and your computer software skills with the other team members is also commendable, since it demonstrates a willingness to contribute to the team spirit. In fact, Kristy said that: he could not have mastered the new database program without your support. In the future, you can improve your speaking skills and your confidence levels if you use this willingness to train others in a more formal setting. One of the goals we've agreed on for the coming year will allow you to do this by presenting a quarterly training session on the software for all new employees.

These comments are effective because:

- They are positive and encouraging to the employee.

- They use others' input to substantiate the supervisor's opinion.

- They indicate areas for development and use the goal-setting process to focus the employee on the future.

Steve, I am pleased to have been your foreman for the last six months of your trial period. You are a capable mechanic, and I value your insight and suggestions on how to make the best repairs we can to the variety of equipment we maintain here at CBX Service Center. Your productivity rating for this period is 84.8 percent. This is an exceptional accomplishment and is 6 percent over your last rating and 9 percent over the divisional goal. As you've suggested and we've agreed upon, your goal for the next rating period will be to achieve a productivity rating of 88 percent.

These comments are effective because:

- They are personal and encouraging.

- They include quantitative performance data that compares the employee's performance to the past.

- They set a new standard that the employee agrees to and which will be motivating to the employee.

Jack, it is essential that you follow the safety procedures outlined in the AMX procedure manual. Safety, for yourself, as well as for the others on your team, is a top priority. Four times this rating period you operated the equipment without your safety goggles. When you do not wear your goggles, you put yourself at risk. In addition, this behavior distracts your coworkers and puts them at risk. As we have discussed previously, continued disregard for this important rule may result in future disciplinary action.

These comments are effective because:

- They include specific examples that show the employee did not meet the expectations for the job.
- They relate the unacceptable behavior to the organization's need.
- They offer specific consequences that will be applied if the behavior does not change.

Mick, your job requires you to prepare detailed, accurate, and timely reports. The department depends on these reports to keep the home office informed of our progress toward our critical goals. These reports are also used to communicate the effectiveness of our marketing efforts to the advertising firm. In short, these reports are critical to the operation of our business and your contribution is highly valued. When the reports are submitted after the monthly deadline, many other people are affected. Twice this quarter, in April and in June, and five times this year (August, October, January, April and June), the reports were submitted at least three days late. After each incident, we discussed the impact of this and you promised to work to meet the deadline in the future. If the reports continue to be late, our division will be affected and your job will be in jeopardy.

We have discussed techniques and methods to be used to avoid the late reports. We have also discussed and documented possible future consequences if the reports continue to be late. For the next three months, I will check with you five days before the due date to assess progress on the report. As we have discussed, another late report will result in a step one disciplinary action.

These comments are effective because:

- They show how unacceptable behavior affects the organization.
- They give specific instances where the behavior was unacceptable.
- They show a pattern of discussion about the issue and show that consequences may follow if the behavior continues.

HOW DO I AVOID SURPRISING THE EMPLOYEE IN THE PERFORMANCE EVALUATION DOCUMENT?

HOT TIP!

Never mention anything in the performance evaluation that has not been discussed in the past.

While the performance evaluation is an appropriate place to discuss poor performance, it is not the place to raise concerns for the first time. Performance evaluations should serve as a summary of all prior performance-related discussions. They are not to be used as a disciplinary tool. Any behavior that is not acceptable should be discussed with the employee immediately after the behavior is displayed. Saving up your concerns for the end of the year is unfair and is not constructive. Depending on the severity of the behavior, it may be appropriate to apply consequences (verbal reprimand, written reprimand, suspension, etc.) when they occur. However, it is never acceptable to use the performance evaluation to inform the employee of problems for the first time. The performance evaluation is not a disciplinary tool!

> *"Surprises" are a cardinal sin. See each business situation for what it is and not through one's emotional glasses of what one might like to think it is.*
>
> —Reginald H. Jones

Performance Checklist

1. Don't begin to write the performance evaluation document until you have gathered all the relevant data.

2. Ask for the employee's feedback and input before writing the evaluation.

3. Use specific examples and active words to describe the employee's behaviors.

4. Phrase performance improvement opportunities as a benefit.

5. Never mention issues in the evaluation that have not been previously discussed.

What Did You Learn?

TRUE OR FALSE QUESTIONS
Circle T or F to indicate whether each of the following statements is true or false.

T   F   1. If the supervisor has kept good documentation throughout the rating period, his/her file should have enough data in it to begin the performance evaluation.

T   F   2. Customers can provide important input into the assessment of an employee's performance.

T   F   3. It is appropriate to give specific examples of an employee's performance in the comments section of the performance evaluation.

T   F   4. Comparing employees to other employees is an effective way to motivate the employee in the performance evaluation document.

MULTIPLE CHOICE QUESTIONS

Circle the letter next to the best answer for each question.

1. Which of the following is the most effective way to let an employee know that he or she needs to be more accurate?

   (a) You are not very accurate with the monthly reports.

   (b) Your monthly reports contain numerous errors.

   (c) You can improve the accuracy of the monthly reports if you double-check the figures before submitting the document to the accounting department.

   (d) You have a problem with accuracy.

2. When writing a performance evaluation document, it is best to:

   (a) Include references to other employees or a coworker's behavior

   (b) Focus on past performance

   (c) Bring up concerns or issues that have never been mentioned before

   (d) Be vague in your language so the employee can make his or her own interpretations

3. Which of the following is *not* the most effective action verb to use when describing an employee's performance?

   (a) Consider

   (b) Guide

   (c) Be able to

   (d) Promote

4. Performance comments should be written in a conversational tone because:

   (a) They develop rapport and commitment from the employee

   (b) They are harder for supervisors to write

   (c) The performance evaluation document should be cold and distant

   (d) None of the above

OBJECTIVE QUESTIONS

1. How does involving employees in the preparation of their performance evaluations by asking for their input create buy-in and commitment to the job?

2. What recommendations would you make to the human resources department and other supervisors in your organization for improving the quality of your written performance evaluations?

Conducting the Evaluation Meeting

The great leaders of tomorrow will be the ones who understand how to get everyone to participate.

—Sara Little Turnbull

This chapter will enable you to:

- Conduct a performance evaluation meeting with confidence.
- Make each performance evaluation meeting a productive experience for you and the employee.
- Ask effective questions of the employee to solicit his or her input and participation during the meeting.
- Follow a format for conducting painless and productive performance evaluation discussions.

The evaluation discussion offers you and the employee a wonderful opportunity. The problem is that most supervisors miss the opportunity entirely! Instead, these meetings are often met with dread and procrastination. Why not approach this meeting with a sense of hope and opportunity?

The painless performance evaluation meeting offers you an approach that will:

- Build employee rapport and respect

- Recognize the employee's achievements

- Thank the employee for his or her efforts

- Encourage the employee to try out new and improved behaviors

- Clarify future performance standards

- Focus on the future

THINK ABOUT IT:

How would you describe the last performance evaluation meeting you conducted? How did you feel when it was over? How do you think the employee felt?

By remembering that the performance evaluation discussion is an opportunity to review the past and plan for the future, you can craft a session that is productive and positive for both you and the employee.

WHAT ARE THE KEY RULES FOR CONDUCTING AN EFFECTIVE PERFORMANCE EVALUATION MEETING?

If your performance evaluation meetings are productive, you should be accomplishing these three objectives:

1. *No Surprises!* No issue should be raised in this meeting that has not been raised in a previous discussion. The performance evaluation meeting is not the place to solve all of the employee's performance challenges. It should be used as a summary of the previous rating period's discussions.

2. *The Employee Talks More than the Supervisor.* By asking questions and listening, rather than reading the evaluation and telling the employee what to do, you will gain buy-in, commitment, and

trust. Remember, performance management is something we do WITH employees, not TO employees! This is a challenge that can be met by following the ideas in this chapter.

3. *Focus on the Future, Not on the Past.*   The past is done. Don't spend too much time discussing the past, and don't emphasize what the employee cannot change. By focusing on the future and discussing future goals and expectations, the tone of the evaluation meeting becomes more hopeful, positive, and productive.

HOT TIP!

By focusing on the future, you encourage the employee to think about changes he or she needs to make.

WHAT SHOULD HAPPEN BEFORE YOU AND THE EMPLOYEE MEET?

Once the performance evaluation document is drafted, you may be tempted to hand it over to the employee and ask for a signature without discussion. Avoid that temptation at all costs! Before you have the performance evaluation discussion with the employee, prepare yourself so that you can guide a positive and productive meeting. Here are a few things you'll want to do before you meet with the employee to discuss the evaluation:

- *Consider the employee's self-evaluation.*   Before you meet with the employee, give the employee's input one last review. Most employees will be conservative in how they view their own performance. However, if you have an employee who seems to view himself or herself more favorably than you do, the self-evaluation can prepare you for this difference in opinion.

HOT TIP!

Do not conduct the performance evaluation discussion without thorough preparation.

- *Prepare for the employee's likely response.*   Before you start talking with the employee about the evaluation, consider the following questions. If you can't answer these questions clearly, you are not ready to discuss performance with the employee.

Questions to Ask Yourself

☑ What are the specific good points on which you will compliment the employee?

☑ What are the specific areas of improvement you intend to discuss?

☑ What reactions do you anticipate? How do you intend to handle these reactions?

☑ Can you support your performance evaluation with factual evidence?

☑ What specific help or corrective action do you expect the employee might need to address performance issues?

☑ What is your approach for gaining acceptance to your suggested corrective action?

☑ What follow-up action do you have in mind?

- *Ask the employee to come prepared with suggestions for future perform-ance goals.*   Part of the evaluation meeting should focus on plan-ning the employee's performance for the future. The employee should play an active role in this process by coming to the meet-ing with these proposed goals. It is the supervisor's job to ask the employee to do this.

- *Meet in a quiet place with no interruptions.*   This seems like a no-brainer, but with all the distractions in our lives, we can't overlook this critical concept. The performance evaluation is the employee's time! He or she expects and deserves uninterrupted feedback and guidance. Eliminate distractions like cell phones, e-mails, or other people. Make sure the location and setting for this meeting is con-ducive to private discussion.

- *Focus on maintaining or improving the employee's self esteem.*   Keep in mind that the goal is not to leave the employee worse than you found him or her. Even though you may have to discuss unpleas-ant subjects, the focus of the conversation should be on how the employee can improve. By focusing on the future, the employee will leave feeling as good, if not better, than when the meeting started.

- *Spend more time listening than speaking.*   This is a big challenge! Supervisors often think it is their job to tell the employee what to do and how to do it. In fact, just the opposite is true in this case. The performance evaluation discus-sion should give the employee a chance to explore options for the fu-ture. If the supervisor is talking, the employee isn't exploring.

> For many people, the answer to the question "What's the opposite of talking?" is "Waiting to talk."
>
> —Susan Scott

- *Focus on development, not control.*   Focus on the employee and what the employee will need to achieve in the future. If you are forcing solutions on the employee, he or she will naturally resist and will be less likely to buy-in to your imposed solutions. Again, ask for input and remember that your job is to help the employee succeed.

- *Use open-ended questions.*   The key to gaining the employee's in-volvement in this discussion is to ask a lot of questions. Be pre-pared not to fill in the silence with your own answers! The next section provides you with possible questions that will encourage the employee to participate more actively in the conversation.

THINK ABOUT IT:

Describe the last performance evaluation meeting you conducted. Did you prepare for the employee's response, ask open-ended questions, and focus on maintaining the employee's self-esteem? What did you do well? What could you have done to improve the meeting?

HOW CAN I ENSURE THAT THE EMPLOYEE KNOWS I'M TAKING THE MEETING SERIOUSLY?

Employees want to know that you are fully focused on them and their performance during the evaluation discussion. Distractions and interruptions send a message to employees that they are not as important as other things. To ensure that you are sending a positive message to the employee that you are fully prepared, consider the items on this checklist.

Evaluation Discussion Preparation Checklist

Have I . . .

- ☑ Chosen a convenient and appropriate setting?
- ☑ Picked a time when both I and the employee can focus on the discussion?
- ☑ Considered how to arrange the room for the meeting?
- ☑ Shared the purpose of the meeting with the employee?
- ☑ Determined the agenda we will follow?
- ☑ Eliminated distractions, including ringing phones, e-mail, or other people?
- ☑ Arranged for coverage so that we will not be interrupted?
- ☑ Planned how I would like the meeting to go?

> Everyone has an invisible sign hanging from his neck saying "Make Me Feel Important!" Never forget this message when working with people.
>
> —Mary Kay Ash

THINK ABOUT IT:

What is the best setting and time to conduct performance evaluations in your office? When are you less likely to be interrupted? What location is most conducive to performance evaluation discussions?

WHAT KINDS OF QUESTIONS SHOULD I ASK THE EMPLOYEE DURING THE PERFORMANCE EVALUATION DISCUSSION?

When asking employees for their view of their performance and of the performance evaluation document, try asking these kinds of questions.

Questions about how the employee views the evaluation

- What did you think about the performance evaluation?
- What surprised you about the evaluation?
- What pleased you most about the evaluation?
- Were there accomplishments or events that were not included that should be included? If so, what were they?

Questions about how the employee views the job

- What do you like most about your job?
- What challenges you most about your job?
- What frustrates you most about your job?
- What could we do next year to make your job more interesting or innovative?
- What could we do next year to make your job less frustrating?
- If you could do one thing to change your job, what would it be?

Questions about how the job and/or workplace can be improved

- How can I help you do your job better?
- What tools would be helpful to you so that you can do a better job?
- What additional resources do you need?
- What could be done to make this a more satisfying workplace?

If those questions are not appropriate for the situation, try the question starters on page 109.

Consider this case study 10, which is a real-life example of what can happen when trying to get an employee involved in the performance evaluation discussion.

Questions Starters

Go on . . .	How could it have been handled better?
Tell me more about . . .	How do you mean?
Give me a typical example . . .	You mentioned previously that . . .
What precisely happened?	Could you remind me again . . . ?
What specifically did you do/say?	Why do you say that?
What was the outcome?	How are you feeling?
What else could have been done?	You said that . . . ?
How did it arise?	How do you see us being able to . . . ?
How did you handle it?	What might happen if . . . ?
How was it resolved?	What did that mean to you?
How often/regularly did this happen?	What if . . . ?
How important/significant is it?	Who else needs to be involved?
How strongly do you feel about it?	

CASE STUDY #10
BUT I DO ALL THE TALKING

Alice is preparing for her upcoming performance evaluation discussion with Cindy, and she is concerned about getting Cindy's input. Cindy is a shy and reserved analyst who does her work with little fanfare. Cindy says little at staff meetings and keeps to herself rather than participating in the department's social events.

Alice is worried that she'll end up doing all the talking during Cindy's performance evaluation and that Cindy will be unwilling to share her perspectives about the job and her ideas for performance goals for the coming year.

- Is Alice's concern a valid one? Why or why not?

- What steps can Alice take to encourage Cindy to participate in the performance evaluation discussion?

WHAT IS THE BEST FORMAT TO FOLLOW FOR THE PERFORMANCE EVALUATION MEETING?

Once you have prepared yourself mentally for the meeting, take time to prepare yourself organizationally. Most evaluation meetings run between thirty and sixty minutes. Depending on the complexity of the job and the level of participation by the employee, the meeting might take longer.

THINK ABOUT IT:

What format do you usually follow when conducting performance evaluation meetings? Does your plan encourage the employee to participate?

This section presents a painless format that is tried and true and will guarantee that the three keys of performance evaluation discussions will be achieved:

- ☑ No surprises!
- ☑ The employee talks more than the supervisor.
- ☑ Focus on the future, not on the past.

The format includes suggested time frames for each step, based on a forty-minute conversation. Notice that more of the discussion time is spent focusing on the future than on rehashing past performance.

Format for Painless Performance Evaluation Discussions

Introduction—2 minutes

- Put the employee at ease.
- The purpose is to have a mutual discussion about how things are going for the employee and to plan for the future.
- Ask if the employee has had a chance to review the draft performance evaluation you have prepared.

Employee's Viewpoint—10 minutes

- Ask the employee to share his or her perspective of the performance and of the performance evaluation.
- Ask how the employee views the job and working climate.

- Ask if the employee has any problems.
- Ask if the employee has any suggestions for improving the job.

   NOTE: This is where you will ask open-ended questions and encourage the employee to share his or her ideas. This is where you listen!!!

Supervisor's Viewpoint—5 minutes

Provide a brief summary of the performance. Remember, this doesn't have to take long because it is already summarized in writing on the evaluation document. Avoid comparing the employee to other employees and focus on the standards for the job and how the employee met or didn't meet the goals and expectations. You might summarize the performance in two parts:

— Behaviors to Continue
   Mention one or two items you appreciate about the employee's work and describe why these behaviors are important to the job.

— Opportunities for Improvement
   Mention any areas for improvement and provide specific examples to support your concerns. Present these as opportunities for improvement rather than shortcomings.

Goals and Objectives for the Coming Year—10 minutes

- Ask the employee to contribute goals and objectives for the next year.
- Discuss goals that will be motivating and challenging for the employee.
- Collaboratively agree on the goals for the coming year.

Training, Development, Further Education Required—5 minutes

- Ask the employee to share training or educational opportunities he or she would like to pursue in the coming year.
- Ask if the employee has any longer term job-related goals you may be able to help him or her reach.

Feedback from the Employee—5 minutes

- Ask the employee how he or she feels about the plan for the coming year.
- Ask if there are questions, concerns, or ideas on how to make the coming year more productive and valuable.
- Let the employee have the last word, even if you don't agree.

Close on a constructive, encouraging note—3 minutes

> *Speaking without thinking is like shooting without aiming.*
> —Old Proverb

HOW CAN YOU CREATE AN ENVIRONMENT WHERE THE EMPLOYEE WILL NOT BECOME DEFENSIVE?

Susan Scott, in her bestseller *Fierce Conversations*, suggests that another tool for describing reality without placing blame is to remove the word *but* from your vocabulary and substitute the word *and*. For example, instead of saying, "I like your idea about the new accounting system, *but* we need to convince Dana to support it" say "I like your idea about the new accounting system, *and* we need to convince Dana to support it."

When we use the word *but*, we negate whatever we've said before it. Substitute the word *and* to open the lines of communication and encourage open-mindedness during the performance evaluation discussion.

> *Premeditate your speeches; words once flown are in the hearer's power, not your own.*
>
> —Anonymous

WHAT DOES A PAINLESS PERFORMANCE EVALUATION SOUND LIKE?

Here's an example of how this conversation might go:

(in the manager's office or an otherwise private place without distractions)

Introduction

Manager: Hi, Peggy. How's it going? Did you get a chance to read the draft of your performance evaluation?

Peggy: Yes, I did. Thanks for giving it to me before the meeting. That gave me time to think about what you've written. I didn't realize I accomplished so much this year.

Manager: Remember, it's still in draft form, so if we need to make any changes, this is the time for us to discuss them. So, what did you think?

Employee's Viewpoint

Peggy: Well, overall it is okay. I was a bit surprised about the mention of my tardiness back in February. I thought we had resolved that.

Manager: Yes, we did resolve it. In fact, I mentioned it in the performance evaluation because you made an effort to correct the problem. Since it was a performance issue that we had to discuss several times throughout the year, it was important to mention it here since the annual evaluation is really a summary of the whole year's performance. You'll notice that I did say that you arrived on time consistently once we discussed the problem.

Peggy: Yes, you did. I guess that's okay then.

Manager: What else did you see in the evaluation that we need to discuss further?

Peggy: I appreciated that you mentioned the fact that I developed the new filing system for the invoices. I had forgotten about that. I also appreciated that you said I worked hard on the Shoemaker case. That was a real challenge this year, and I don't think I could have gotten it done without Jay's support. I hope we never have a case like that one in the future.

Manager: Yes, that was definitely a highlight for you. Was there anything in the evaluation that concerned you?

Peggy: No, not really.

Manager: Is there anything you think we can do to improve the job in any way?

Peggy: Oh, I don't know. I really haven't thought about it.

Manager: I'm sure there is something you would like to see changed that would make your day-to-day work more efficient.

Peggy: Well, I would like to have more time to analyze the case loads, rather than plowing through them without thinking. I know it's tough because we have the vacant position, but if I only had an extra hour or two a day, I know I would be more effective and the quality of the work would improve.

Manager: How do you think we can accomplish that?

Peggy: If David would be willing to do the legal reviews, that would free me up a little more.

Manager: That's an interesting idea. Let's make a note of that and talk to David about it tomorrow. I would be willing to move things around if you think it would allow you to be more thorough.

Peggy: Thanks!

Manager: Anything else?

Peggy: No, not that I can think of.

Supervisor's Viewpoint

Manager: To summarize, as I noted on the evaluation, you have done a great job with the difficult cases that have been assigned to you. The Shoemaker case and the Kirschbaum case were particularly tough. Thanks for your diligence in resolving these issues. You also have excelled in the development of new procedures for the office. Since you implemented the new tracking system, everyone in the office is less frustrated.

And, in the coming year, you can enhance your customer relations skills by giving more attention to the detail of your case files. A little more time spent making sure the forms are filled out correctly will help to bring your work to a higher level. Having David handle the legal reviews will probably help in this area. Also, if you are struggling with a difficult customer or coworker, please let me know before it becomes an issue.

Peggy: Okay, I understand these are issues that I need to look at.

Goals and Objectives for the Coming Year

Manager: Great. Let's talk about the coming year. What goals have you been thinking would be appropriate for you to focus on for the next year?

Peggy: Well, I prepared this list of goals. First, I would like to attend a class in Microsoft Access so that I can better manipulate the customer database. I would also like to cross-train with Lauren to learn how to track the invoices using her system. Of course, I also listed our regular goals like the number of customers we are to meet each day and the sales quotas that we all have.

Manager: It sounds like you put some thought into this. Thanks for thinking ahead. I had a few goals in mind as well. We are moving toward an electronic case file system this year. With that in mind, I'd like to see you take the lead in learning the system and then serving as a coach for your coworkers.

Peggy: I don't know if I can do that. I've never coached anyone before and I don't know the software.

Manager: That's why I would like for one of your goals to be to attend the training and to develop a tutorial for the staff.

Peggy: Well, if you give me the time to do it, I guess I could try it.

Manager: Of course you'll be given the time. How much time do you think you'll need and what adjustments to your work load do you think we might need to make?

Peggy: I'm not sure, but I may need my quotas lowered during the months that I'm working on it.

Manager: We can do that. Let's talk about it when we have our project planning meeting next week.

Peggy: Okay.

Training, Development, Further Education Required

Manager: Is there other training you'd like to receive this year? Any developmental opportunities you'd like to explore?

Peggy: Not that I can think of. Attending the Microsoft Access class and learning the new case file software should be enough.

Manager: I agree. That's a lot on your plate so far. Do you have any long-term career goals that I may be able to help you reach?

Peggy: I'm really content working here. Every day is a new challenge.

Manager: That's fine. If you change your mind and decide that you would like to go in a new direction, let me know and I'll see what I can do to help.

Feedback from the Employee

Manager: So, how do you feel about the plan we've laid out for the coming year?

Peggy: I think it will be challenging, but I'm excited to get started.

Manager: Do you have any questions, concerns, or ideas on how we can make the coming year more productive?

Peggy: No, not really. I think we are headed in the right direction.

Close on a Constructive, Encouraging Note

Manager: Well, if anything else comes to mind, please don't hesitate to bring the idea to me. My goal is to help you be successful here. I'll finalize the forms and sign it. Don't forget to write your own comments and sign the form after that. Thanks for your time today.

Peggy: Thanks!

Performance Checklist

1. Spend time preparing for the performance evaluation discussion.

2. Anticipate the employee's response to the performance evaluation document.

3. Ensure that your evaluation discussions include no surprises, include opportunities for the employee to share his or her ideas, and focus on the future.

4. Use open-ended questions to foster discussion during the evaluation discussion.

5. Follow a format to guide and manage the flow of the discussion.

What Did You Learn?

TRUE OR FALSE QUESTIONS
Circle T or F to indicate whether each of the following statements is true or false.

T   F   1. The employee's view of his or her performance is not relevant to the performance evaluation discussion.

T   F   2. Performance evaluation discussions should spend more time focusing on the future than rehashing the past.

T   F   3. The supervisor should do most of the talking in a performance evaluation discussion.

T   F   4. The performance evaluation discussion is the opportunity for the supervisor to share observations he or she has been saving up all year.

MULTIPLE CHOICE QUESTIONS
Circle the letter next to the best answer for each question.

1. The key to an effective performance evaluation discussion is:
   (a) The employee talks more than the supervisor
   (b) There are no surprises to the employee
   (c) The focus of the discussion is on the future
   (d) All of the above

2. In preparing for the performance evaluation discussion, the supervisor should consider which of the following?
   (a) How the employee's paycheck will be affected
   (b) How the employee is likely to react to the performance evaluation document

(c) How the supervisor will defend himself or herself if the employee disagrees

(d) None of the above

3. Which of the following is *not* an appropriate question to ask when soliciting the employee's view of his or her performance?

(a) What pleased you most about the evaluation?

(b) What can I do to help you?

(c) Why are you not as productive as Heidi?

(d) What frustrates you most about your job?

4. Which of the following is not an element of a painless performance evaluation discussion?

(a) The supervisor does all the talking.

(b) The employee's view is solicited.

(c) The supervisor and the employee discuss and agree upon goals and objectives for the coming rating period.

(d) The employee has the last word.

OBJECTIVE QUESTIONS

1. How can you ensure that the painless performance evaluation format is followed during the discussion with the employee? How can a supervisor keep this discussion on track and focused?

2. What are the benefits of involving the employee in the performance evaluation discussion by asking open-ended questions?

Encouraging Employees to Participate in the Performance Management Process

Build your reputation by helping other people build theirs.

—Anthony J. D'Angelo

This chapter will enable you to:

- Involve your employees in the performance management process.

- Gain valuable input from employees throughout the rating period.

- Solicit employee comments on the performance evaluation document that are meaningful and useful.

- Guide employees as they participate in the performance management cycle.

Employees play a critical role in the entire performance management process. You can improve your chances of success when conducting a painless performance evaluation if your employees are also aware of the approach you are using. Remember, performance management is something we do WITH employees, not TO employees. Helping them to understand their role will enable them to fully participate in the process.

HOT TIP!

Check your attitude! What you believe about performance management will be passed on to your employees.

HOW DO I ENCOURAGE MY EMPLOYEES TO PARTICIPATE IN THE MANAGEMENT OF THEIR OWN PERFORMANCE?

Your approach and attitude toward performance management will set the tone for how employees see the process. If you view performance management as an opportunity for enhanced communication and dialogue with employees, your employees are more likely to view it as an opportunity as well. If you dread the process and procrastinate each step, employees are also likely to avoid taking responsibility for their role in the performance management process.

THINK ABOUT IT:

When performance evaluation time rolls around, how do employees feel about the process? How do your actions contribute to their beliefs about performance management?

You can make your expectations known by discussing them with employees at staff meetings and during one-on-one meetings. You may also want to provide your employees with tools to help them feel more comfortable participating in their own performance management. This chapter recommends such tools.

Employees will only participate in the management of their own performance if they know you expect them to do so. Use every opportunity available to you to share your expectations about their participation in the performance evaluation process.

THINK ABOUT IT:

How can you encourage your employees to take a more active role in the performance management process?

Here is a checklist you can share with employees that will help them to understand the role they play. Copy this checklist and share it with your staff.

> Don't assume that the interests of employer and employee are necessarily hostile. . . . The opposite is more apt to be the case.
>
> —Louis Dembitz Brandeis

Tips for Employees: Participating in the Management of Your Own Performance

- ☑ Take the self-evaluation opportunity seriously and contribute as much specific and detailed information about your performance as possible. Include examples of your work and reminders of projects you have completed throughout the rating period.

- ☑ Be honest in your evaluation of your performance. Note the highlights and the lowlights of the previous rating period. If you are honest with yourself, your supervisor will be more likely to look for ways to help you improve.

- ☑ Keep your own performance file or a "me" file. Record examples of tough projects you've completed and goals you've achieved.

- ☑ Keep your supervisor informed of your performance successes and challenges throughout the rating period.

- ☑ When asked to offer ideas for performance goals, remember to be specific, measurable, realistic, and time-oriented in what you propose.

- ☑ Come to the performance evaluation meeting prepared to discuss your ideas in a productive way.

- ☑ Accept constructive feedback that will help you to be more effective on the job. If the supervisor does not provide specific examples of how you can improve, ask for help in a productive manner.

- ☑ Offer ideas for professional development goals you would like to pursue in the coming year.

- ☑ Take time to write complete and thoughtful comments on the evaluation. Comments are your opportunity to have your perspectives documented. Use comments to your fullest advantage.

HOW CAN I ENCOURAGE EMPLOYEES TO KEEP ME INFORMED OF THEIR PERFORMANCE PROGRESS THROUGHOUT THE RATING PERIOD?

Frequent and informal feedback throughout the rating period is critical to effective performance management. Employees need to understand that you expect them to share with you their successes and their challenges along the way. You can encourage such sharing through:

☑ Weekly or monthly check-up meetings (face to face, on the phone, via conference call, etc.)

☑ Weekly or monthly written reports

☑ Frequent e-mails and phone calls between you and the employee to share incidents and situations that occur on the job

☑ A performance log that you keep to record situations the employee experiences throughout the rating period

☑ A request that employees maintain a "me" file, a place where they can keep their own records about their performance

HOT TIP!

Make sure employees know that you expect them to fully participate in the management of their own performance.

THINK ABOUT IT:

What do you do to encourage employees to continually share their job experiences with you?

If there's any single mistake that people make about holding on to their jobs, it's a failure to communicate with the boss. I know the term "communication" is sometimes awkward, but I can't emphasize enough how important it is to let your boss know what you're doing.

—S. Eric Wachtel

By letting employees know that you are interested in their work experience and by asking for their perspectives and ideas, you will create a work environment of strong communication and dialogue.

HOW CAN I ENCOURAGE EMPLOYEES TO WRITE USEFUL AND MEANINGFUL COMMENTS ON THE PERFORMANCE EVALUATION DOCUMENT?

Most performance evaluation documents include a section where employees can share their comments and perspectives about the evaluation. Employees often do not know what to write in the comments section of the performance evaluation document because they have not been given the necessary guidance to make the most of this opportunity. Have you ever gotten a performance evaluation back from an employee with a "no comment" written in the employee comments section? This reply is not unusual, especially if employees do not understand the value of their comments. They will look to you for guidance on how to use this part of the evaluation to their advantage. Consider this case when encouraging employees to share their views.

CASE STUDY #11
I DON'T KNOW AND I DON'T CARE

Zach is a machine operator who comes to work, does his job, and goes home each day without much fanfare. He is an effective worker, but he is not overly creative and often seems detached from his work.

Zach's annual performance evaluation is due soon and as his supervisor, you want to make sure his input is heard and included. In the past, when you have asked him for input via a self-evaluation form, Zach has provided little input. When you have conducted past evaluation meetings, Zach has had little to offer in terms of ideas for how to improve the job or how to make it more satisfying. In fact, there was quite a bit of silence during the evaluation discussion.

You are now giving Zach a copy of this year's evaluation and are requesting that he include his comments on the form so that his views are documented and heard. You know that he is not fully satisfied with the overall rating and that he has opinions about the job since you've heard him express his view to his coworkers. You expect to receive a "no comment" on the evaluation form when it comes back from Zach even though you know that Zach has opinions and ideas to share.

- What can you do to encourage Zach to provide thoughtful and detailed comments?

- What steps can you take if Zach provides little or no feedback on the evaluation? Should you ask him to be more detailed and specific?

- How important is it that Zach participates in the management of his own performance?

HOT TIP!

Encourage employees to honestly contribute their ideas in the comments section of the performance evaluation document.

Zach's case is not unusual. However, Zach may not understand his options for using the comments section to his advantage. Here are some tips that you might want to copy and share with your employees to give them direction on how to use the employee comments section productively.

The following tips may be appropriate to share with your employees when you are encouraging them to participate in the performance management process.

Tips for Employees: Writing Your Performance Evaluation Comments

Writing comments on your own performance evaluation is sometimes challenging. Learn to respond to your evaluation by considering these tips:

☑ Read the performance evaluation document carefully. Don't respond immediately; give yourself at least a day to think about the comments and ratings before you write your comments. Nothing gets handled well in the heat of the moment.

☑ Acknowledge points where there is agreement.

☑ Use clear examples to contradict those points that you feel are not justified. Without specific and clear examples it is hard to prove your point.

☑ Complete sentences are not necessary. Write in any way that gets your point across clearly.

☑ Keep a file of the important aspects of your job so that you can give specific examples. This "me" file will help you discuss your performance with your supervisor.

☑ Acknowledge your supervisor, coworkers, or other people who gave you support or guidance throughout the rating period.

☑ Balance your comments with positive and constructive ideas.

☑ Remember, your comments will not be used against you. This is your opportunity to express yourself.

☑ Keep an open mind. The performance evaluation is an opportunity to reflect on the past and plan for the future. Use it to your benefit.

If you want to move up in business, the first rule is not to be invisible. . . . To be noticed by bosses, do ask questions and offer constructive advice. Don't substitute talk for action. Don't be afraid to present your best abilities when the opportunity arrives. Don't be shy.

—George Mazzei

Here is another list of ideas you may share with employees to encourage them to write thoughtful and meaningful comments on the performance evaluation document.

Tips for Employees: Start Your Comments with . . .

Here are a few ideas for starting your comments on your own performance evaluation document:

- ☑ "Thank you for acknowledging/noticing/commenting on . . . "
- ☑ "I am glad I had the experience of working on . . . "
- ☑ "I enjoy my job and the _____ it provides me."
- ☑ "I would like to make note of my low sick leave use of _____ hours for this rating period."
- ☑ "My leave time increased this rating period due to . . . "
- ☑ "I agree/disagree with the ratings/comments on my performance evaluation since I have . . . "

HOW DO I ENCOURAGE EMPLOYEES TO FULLY PARTICIPATE IN THE ENTIRE PERFORMANCE MANAGEMENT PROCESS?

Don't be afraid to share the concepts of performance management with employees. They should understand that performance management is a continuous process that requires their full participation. Share with them that frequent and informal feedback throughout the rating period is critical. Let them know that you will be keeping thorough records to document their performance successes and challenges. Encourage them to keep the same kinds of records for themselves. These records will be essential when the time comes to write the year-end performance evaluation document.

> *The deepest principle in human nature is the craving to be appreciated.*
>
> —William James

Most of all, remind employees that performance management is a process that is of great benefit to them. It leads to clearer expectations, strong communication, and ideally, no surprises at performance evaluation time.

Performance Checklist

1. Tell employees they have an opportunity to participate in the management of their own performance.

2. Meet regularly with employees to encourage them to share performance successes and challenges.

3. Help employees understand how to fully use the employee comments section on the performance evaluation document.

4. Create a work environment based on strong communication and dialogue by encouraging employees to participate in the management of their own performance.

What Did You Learn?

TRUE OR FALSE QUESTIONS

Circle T or F to indicate whether each of the following statements is true or false.

T   F   1. Employees should be encouraged to sit back and allow the performance management process to happen to them.

T   F   2. Employees should keep a "me" file to record examples of their performance so that they can share it with the supervisor at the end of the rating period.

T   F   3. Employees should be expected to offer ideas for performance goals to be pursued in the future.

T   F   4. Employee comments should be used against the employee if they are negative or if the employee does not agree with the supervisor.

MULTIPLE CHOICE QUESTIONS

Circle the letter next to the best answer for each question.

1. When employees are writing comments on their own performance evaluation document, they should be encouraged to:

(a) Wait a day or two to think about the supervisor's rating instead of writing from their first gut reaction.

(b) Write only "no comment."

(c) Focus only on areas where they disagree with the supervisor's evaluation.

(d) Provide excuses for all the problems they have had during the rating period.

2. Effective employee comments may start with all of the following except:

(a) I'm glad I had the experience of working on . . .

(b) I enjoy my job because . . .

(c) My supervisor has made a poor judgment related to my work on X project.

(d) I agree/disagree with the ratings on my performance evaluation since I have . . .

3. Employees can be encouraged to take a more active role in the management of their performance by:

(a) Thoroughly completing the self-evaluation for the supervisor

(b) Saving up their complaints to the supervisor and sharing them during the performance evaluation discussion

(c) Avoiding any constructive feedback that may improve performance

(d) None of the above

4. The benefits to the employee of participating in their own performance management include all but which of the following?

(a) Enhanced communication between the employee and supervisor

(b) Clear expectations

(c) No surprises during the evaluation discussion

(d) A chance to tell the supervisor that they think the supervisor is ineffective

OBJECTIVE QUESTIONS

1. What can supervisors do to create an environment where employees will fully participate in the management of their performance on a daily basis?

2. What are the results of a work environment that does not encourage employees to fully participate in the management of their performance? How would you describe such a work environment?

Important Terms

Americans with Disabilities Act of 1990 (ADA)—Title I of the ADA prohibits discrimination in hiring based on disability or perceived disability.

Attitude—An individual's perspective, thoughts, or belief about an issue, situation, or person. Attitudes are internal thoughts and/or feelings that underlie a person's actions.

Behavior—The actions or reactions of a person in response to external or internal stimuli. Behaviors are observable things people say, do, or do not say or do.

Documentation—The act or an instance of the supplying of documents or supporting references or records; confirmation that some fact or statement is true.

Employee self-evaluation—The employee's perspective about his or her performance, usually submitted to the supervisor prior to the formal performance evaluation and used as input by the supervisor.

Goal—A job-related task or activity the employee is expected to achieve that is specific, measurable, attainable, agreed upon, realistic, and time-oriented.

Job description—The official document, usually maintained by the human resources department, that defines the essential functions, duties, and responsibilities of the job.

"Me" file—The file an employee keeps related to his or her own performance that documents the performance from the employee's perspective.

Performance—The carrying into execution or action a duty or task; performance is usually measured in achievement or accomplishment, represented by an action. Performance is how the person does his or her job.

Performance evaluation—Also referred to as *performance appraisal* or *performance review*, the formalized process of documenting performance on a regular basis and providing feedback to an employee about performance successes and challenges.

Performance log—A standardized form on which a supervisor maintains an ongoing record of an employee's performance.

Performance management—The process of providing direction, feedback, and recognition to an employee in an organizational setting.

Performance management cycle—The ongoing process of setting clear expectations, providing feedback, and documenting an employee's performance.

Performance management system—An organization-wide process that establishes short- and long-term goals for the organization, for departments, for work units, and for individuals.

Performance planning—The first step in the performance management cycle where the employee and supervisor work together to establish goals and expectations for the employee's performance.

Rating form—Also referred to as the *performance evaluation document*, the organization-specific form that a supervisor uses to complete a performance evaluation.

Rating period—The period of time for which an employee will be evaluated using a performance evaluation system. Rating periods can be one quarter, one year, or any other time period the organization establishes.

Rating scale—Also referred to as *rating categories*, a grading system that typically uses letters or numbers to describe an employee's performance.

Recency error—The tendency to base a performance evaluation on the most recent events in your memory and to exclude past events or incidents you do not remember.

What Did You Learn? Answer Key and Case Study Responses

CHAPTER ONE: INTRODUCTION TO PERFORMANCE MANAGEMENT

True or False Questions:
1. True
2. True
3. True
4. False

Multiple Choice Questions:
1. C
2. A
3. D
4. A

CASE STUDY #1: PROBATION?

Has this ever happened in your organization?

If your organization has a trial period at the beginning of a new employee's tenure, it is likely this situation has happened. Supervisors often avoid giving honest and direct feedback to employees in hopes that the unwanted behavior will improve on its own. This "ostrich effect" of looking away and hoping that the person will change, rarely, if ever, works.

What are the potential consequences of letting the employee pass the trial period?

If the supervisor allows the new employee to pass the probationary period, he or she will be faced with several challenges in the future. First, by not addressing the employee's behavior, the supervisor has essentially endorsed the behavior and thus has lowered the standards for the entire work unit. The new employee's poor performance, messy work habits, and tardiness have now become the norm. Also, in many organizations, once employees pass the trial period, they earn certain employment rights. Such rights may be established by a union contract or a civil service system if the organization is in the public sector. Once an employee earns these rights, it may be more difficult to terminate him or her, due to elaborate documentation requirements and progressive discipline steps. Finally, if the supervisor approves the employee's probation, the supervisor risks earning a reputation as being someone who does not make good hires. The trial period should be considered part of the hiring process. If the supervisor sees that the employee is not meeting standards within the trial period, the employee should be counseled early and terminated if the performance does not improve.

What are the potential consequences of addressing the behaviors at this point?

The greatest risk of addressing the employee's messy work habits and tardiness is that the employee may be surprised and angry that the supervisor did not address the issues earlier. The supervisor should gain the support of his or her manager and/or the human resources department to ensure that the situation is addressed fairly and legally.

CASE STUDY #2: THE INHERITED EMPLOYEE

Has this ever happened in your organization?

Depending on the size of your organization, it is likely that you have inherited employees who need to improve their performance. If you are assigned to supervise a work group you have never supervised, then you will likely inherit the staff that is in place when you arrive. If so, it is not uncommon to find that the previous supervisors were not thorough in their documentation.

What predicament might you face if her behavior does not change and you resort to disciplinary action?

If her behavior continues, it should be addressed. First, the new supervisor should establish clear expectations for all employees. If there are specific concerns, it is best for the supervisor to discuss these concerns as early as possible to give the employee a chance to improve. Should the employee continue the inappropriate work behaviors after the supervisor has made the expectations clear, disciplinary action will likely be the next step.

What are the potential consequences of not addressing the behavior, as it appears the previous supervisors have done?

If the new supervisor decides to ignore the tardiness, rudeness, and sloppy work, those behaviors are essentially endorsed. As soon as the other employees in the work unit see that the supervisor is not holding the clerk accountable for her behaviors, they will lose respect for the supervisor and/or they will adapt their behaviors to meet the new, lower standard set by the clerk.

CHAPTER TWO: NAVIGATING THE PERFORMANCE MANAGEMENT PROCESS

True or False Questions:
1. True
2. True
3. False
4. True

Multiple Choice Questions:
1. D
2. A
3. B
4. D

CASE STUDY #3: MISSING A STEP

What step in the performance management process has Hannah overlooked?

Hannah is not meeting frequently and informally with each employee to provide feedback and guidance. She is also not keeping regular notes and documentation about their performance.

How does leaving a step out affect Hannah's relationship with her employees?

By not providing regular feedback to her employees, Hannah sends a message to them that she does not have time for them or that they are not important to her. As a result, employees feel neglected and complain about the lack of feedback. In the long run, a lack of feedback can create low morale and increased grievances. Hannah is also likely to see more complaints and appeals about the annual performance evaluations because employees will be surprised to hear her feedback.

What would you recommend to Hannah in this situation?

Hannah should begin meeting with each employee on a one-to-one, face-to-face basis to discuss how his or her job is going. In these informal discussions, Hannah can provide praise, recognition, and support to her employees. She can also redirect those who may not be fully productive. She should keep notes about each of these discussions so that at the end of the rating period, she has a complete record of the employee's performance that reflects the entire rating period.

CHAPTER THREE: CLARIFYING PERFORMANCE EXPECTATIONS AND SETTING GOALS

True or False Questions:

1. True
2. False
3. True
4. False

Multiple Choice Questions:

1. B
2. D
3. C
4. A

CASE STUDY #4: CLEAN SHRIMP

Why did Michael misunderstand Margaret's expectation?

Without knowing Michael's background and training, it is easy to see that Margaret made an assumption about Michael's skills and knowledge. Making an assumption about what the other person knows or does not know can be dangerous to a supervisor trying to make his or her expectations clear.

What steps could Margaret have taken to ensure·that Michael understood her request?

Margaret could have asked Michael to share his plan of attack with her. Margaret could have asked, "How have you gone about cleaning shrimp in the past?" This kind of open-ended question would give Michael the opportunity to share his perspectives and experiences with Margaret. Margaret could have also checked in with Michael at regular intervals to make sure he was progressing successfully.

How can Margaret ensure that Michael is successful in the future?

Margaret can use the success factors described in the chapter to make sure that Michael understands her expectations. She can explain the success criteria for Michael by saying, "This project will be successful if. . . ." She can provide interim progress reports to Michael by checking in on him regularly while he completes the task. She may also ask Michael to explain the task to her before he begins.

CHAPTER FOUR: DOCUMENTING PERFORMANCE FAIRLY AND LEGALLY

True or False Questions:

1. True
2. False
3. False
4. False

Multiple Choice Questions:

1. C
2. A
3. C
4. D

CASE STUDY #5: A BLANK SHEET OF PAPER

Can David discuss the past incidents with Sam, based on his own experiences, even if they are not documented by the previous supervisor? Why or why not?

David can mention the previous incidents; however, it is best that he focus on the future. Rehashing the past does no one any good. David should talk with Sam about his expectations that include meeting deadlines and preparing accurate work. David may mention past situations as a way of letting Sam know that these standards are a high priority. However, David would be wise to avoid holding Sam accountable for the past when David was not in a position to do so.

Where should David begin in terms of the documentation?

David should begin by documenting his expectations for Sam's performance. He should put his expectations in writing and share them with Sam openly and honestly. David may even want to get Sam's signature on the expectations to ensure there is a record that Sam is aware of David's expectations.

How relevant is David's memory of past incidents to the situation? Can he document his past experiences now?

David's memory is relevant in that it will help him be clear about his expectations for the future. However, Sam deserves to be given a chance to improve his performance, and their discussions should be focused on the future. David cannot document his past experiences, especially if they were never discussed with Sam at the time the incidents occurred.

CHAPTER FIVE: MAKING PERFORMANCE MANAGEMENT A PRIORITY

True or False Questions:

1. False
2. False
3. True
4. True

Multiple Choice Questions:

1. A
2. D
3. C
4. D

CASE STUDY #6: FINDING TIME TO DO THE RIGHT THING

What impact would regular feedback meetings with employees have on this manager's effectiveness as a leader?

Regular feedback meetings would allow this manager to develop rapport and trust with his employees. By meeting on a regular basis, the employees will have the opportunity to hear his support and to ask him for guidance on tough projects. Regular meetings with individual employees will likely enhance their morale and commitment to the workplace because they feel supported and recognized.

What can this manager do to help his employees feel that they are fully supported?

The manager must meet with each employee on a weekly or monthly basis to discuss their progress toward performance goals and to talk about the challenges they are facing on the job. By regularly communicating, the employees will know that they can count on their manager for support and clarity of direction.

How can this manager ensure that he has the time to make his performance expectations clear for every employee?

The manager should make time on his schedule to meet with each employee for a short time each month. Weekly meetings are even better. These meetings should be scheduled and the time should be protected from conflicts or other pressing priorities. There will always be something else to do. By making individual meetings with each employee a priority, the employee learns that his or her work and efforts are appreciated.

CHAPTER SIX: IDENTIFYING AND ADDRESSING PERFORMANCE ISSUES

True or False Questions:

1. False
2. True
3. True
4. False

Multiple Choice Questions

1. C
2. D
3. B
4. D

CASE STUDY #7: SUSAN AND THE SEASONED ENGINEER

Is Susan's concern about Elyse's behavior a legitimate performance issue or a personal pet peeve?

It is likely that Susan's concern is a pet peeve. As long as Elyse is ready to work at her agreed-upon start time, what she does before and after those work hours are not relevant to Susan.

What are the potential consequences if Susan addresses the issue with Elyse?

If Susan were to address the issue with Elyse, she is likely to damage the relationship between the two of them. If Susan cannot link Elyse's slow entrance to the office with her ability to perform the job duties, it will be hard for her to justify a request that Elyse change her behavior. Susan should focus on Elyse's performance and should ask herself if it is worth it to raise this issue. Some battles are not worth fighting.

What would you recommend to Susan about this situation?

Susan should forget about the situation and focus on what Elyse is doing well. If Elyse's arrival time begins to impact her ability to complete her work assignments, then Susan may justifiably talk with Elyse about her lateness and its impact on the work unit. Otherwise, Susan should focus on more relevant and productive issues.

CHAPTER SEVEN: RATING PERFORMANCE OBJECTIVELY AND LEGALLY

True or False Questions:

1. True
2. False
3. True
4. False

Multiple Choice Questions:

1. C
2. B
3. D
4. C

CASE STUDY #8: THE NEW, ENTHUSIASTIC ASSOCIATE

How should Lorraine respond to Wayne's tough question?

Lorraine should be ready to give Wayne specific examples of workplace behaviors that represent each level of the rating categories. If she is not prepared to give such an explanation, she should be honest with Wayne and ask him to help her define each level. It is also recommended that Lorraine document her expectations related to each rating level and share those with all employees.

If Wayne does not receive the highest rating in every category on the form, does this mean that he has "failed" on the job? How would you explain your rationale to Wayne?

It is important for Lorraine to explain that it is unlikely that Wayne will get the highest rating in every category. She can explain that the middle rating on the form is labeled as it is (Successful, Meets Expectations, Satisfactory, etc.) because it represents what employees are expected to do. To earn this rating means that the employee has done his or her job well.

What steps would you recommend to Lorraine in addressing Wayne's question?

Lorraine should not enter into a conversation with an employee about the performance evaluation ratings until she has it clear in her mind what the differences in each rating level means. She might ask for help from the employees in defining each level for the specific jobs performed in the work unit. If Lorraine is expected to rate employees using a rating scale, it is critical that she be able to clearly explain the scale to others in behavioral terms.

CHAPTER EIGHT: WRITING THE PERFORMANCE EVALUATION DOCUMENT

True or False Questions:

1. True
2. True
3. True
4. False

Multiple Choice Questions:

1. C
2. B
3. C
4. A

CASE STUDY #9: HOW CAN I SAY THIS?

What concerns do you have about the comments that George has prepared?

The comments prepared by George lack specific examples to illustrate Carol's performance. In addition, the comments are written in the third person voice, which is cold and distant. George also compares Carol to other employees when he says that she is not the top performer in the department. The statement that "Carol can improve by making sure she meets her customers' needs" is vague and unclear.

What are the likely results if George submits these comments to Carol on her performance evaluation?

If George submits these comments to Carol, he will be missing an opportunity to identify specific behaviors he'd like to see her change, and he will likely demotivate her by not showing interest in helping her succeed. The short, vague comments will not be helpful to Carol, nor will they be of value to anyone else who may supervise Carol in the future.

Rewrite the comments on Carol's performance evaluation so that the comments are more specific and constructive.

George can rewrite the comments to be more specific and productive. Here's an example of how George might better use this opportunity:

> Carol, during this rating period you have been effective in responding to a high volume of customer calls. In fact, your average call completion rate was 300 calls per week. And, while call volume is important, so is call quality and customer satisfaction. This rating period you received an average of 10 customer complaints per week. Most of the complaints related to your ability to address the customer's unique concerns. You can improve your call quality by slowing down to ensure that each customer's needs are met before hanging up to answer the next call. The quality of each call is as important as the number of calls you handle.

CHAPTER NINE: CONDUCTING THE EVALUATION MEETING

True or False Questions:

1. False
2. True
3. False
4. False

Multiple Choice Questions:

1. D
2. B
3. C
4. A

CASE STUDY #10: BUT I DO ALL THE TALKING

Is Alice's concern a valid one? Why or why not?

Alice's concern is valid because she knows that Cindy has useful, insightful ideas about how to do her job better. While it might take more patience and persistence than Alice typically uses, she should make an effort to encourage Cindy to participate in the management of her own performance.

What steps can Alice take to encourage Cindy to participate in the performance evaluation discussion?

Alice may consider a number of steps in trying to get Cindy to participate, including:

- Asking Cindy to prepare some performance goals in writing before they meet
- Encouraging Cindy to actively participate and letting her know that her input is valued
- Asking open-ended questions of Cindy that solicit her views about the evaluation, the job, and the future
- Tolerating Cindy's silence after a question has been asked and by being patient for Cindy's response

CHAPTER TEN: ENCOURAGING EMPLOYEES TO PARTICIPATE IN THE PERFORMANCE MANAGEMENT PROCESS

True or False Questions:

1. False
2. True
3. True
4. False

Multiple Choice Questions:

1. A
2. C
3. A
4. D

CASE STUDY #11: I DON'T KNOW AND I DON'T CARE

What can you do to encourage Zach to provide thoughtful and detailed comments?

The supervisor can explain to Zach that the performance evaluation is a place to be heard and that his comments will not be judged. He needs to be reassured that he will not be punished for being honest. The supervisor may also want to provide Zach with some tools for providing comments on the evaluation form. Finally, the supervisor may want to ask open-ended questions of Zach to draw out his opinions.

What steps can you take if Zach provides little or no feedback on the evaluation? Should you ask him to be more detailed and specific?

If Zach provides little or no feedback on the performance evaluation, it is not inappropriate to ask him to write a little more. Ask him to be specific and detailed. However, if Zach refuses to write more information on the form, it is not the supervisor's responsibility to force the issue. The supervisor's job is to create an environment where employees feel comfortable sharing their views. If employees choose not to share their ideas, the supervisor should not force them to do so or penalize them for not doing so.

How important is it that Zach participates in the management of his own performance?

The more Zach participates in the management of his own performance, the more control he will feel over his job. He will likely be more engaged on the job because he is taking ownership in its direction. Zach may not be participating in the management of his performance because he had not been asked to do so in the past. It may take time and patience, but encouraging Zach to participate in the performance-related discussion will enhance his commitment to the job.

Sample Performance Management Tools

The following forms provide one example of formats that are typically used throughout the performance management cycle.

Every organization will have its own forms and process to reflect the organization's policies and practices.

THREE-MONTH EMPLOYEE ORIENTATION FEEDBACK SUMMARY

Complete this form with an employee who is on a six-month trial or probationary status. The form should be used to foster communication and feedback with the employee part way through the trial period.

Employee:	Job Title:
Department:	Rating from: to:
Supervisor:	Reviewer:

Performance strengths exhibited in the first three months:

Areas for continued growth and development:

Based on your performance in the first three months in this position, you

❏ are making acceptable progress toward becoming a regular employee.*

❏ are not making acceptable progress toward becoming a regular employee.

Action items and/or expected performance outcomes necessary to successfully complete the orientation period:

Employee's Comments (attach additional page):

Employee's signature:	Date:
Supervisor's signature:	Date:

Distribution: Employee   Supervisor   HR-Personnel File

*Acceptable progress today does not guarantee satisfactory completion of the orientation period.

ORIENTATION PERIOD PERFORMANCE EVALUATION

Use this form to provide feedback to an employee who is completing the probationary/trial period and whose employee status will change as a result of this evaluation.

Employee:	Job Title:
Department:	Rating from: to:
Supervisor:	Reviewer:

Performance strengths exhibited during the orientation period:

Areas for continued growth and development:

Based on your performance during this orientation period,

❑ you have successfully completed your orientation period and are now a regular status employee, effective __/__/__.

❑ your orientation period has been extended ___ days. (Performance Improvement Plan Required)

❑ you have failed to successfully complete your orientation period.

Professional Development Goals Planned for Next Six Months: Goals should be written in a specific, measurable, attainable, agreed upon, realistic, and time-oriented manner.	Rank order goals in order of priority (1, 2, 3)

COMMENTS AND SIGNATURES

Supervisor's Comments (or attach additional page)

Employee's Comments (or attach additional page) Employee has five days to complete their comments and may choose to write "no comment."

Employee's signature:	Date:
Supervisor's signature:	Date:
Reviewer's signature:	Date:
Human resource staff signature:	Date:

EMPLOYEE PERFORMANCE EVALUATION

Use this form to summarize and document an employee's performance on an annual or more frequent basis.

Employee:	Job Title:
Department:	Rating from: to:
Supervisor:	Reviewer (supervisor's supervisor):
Type of Review: ❏ Annual Review	❏ Other:

Directions: Each factor should be rated for each employee. Comments are required for performance rated at a 1 or 5 level and are suggested for all ratings.

SECTION I: PERFORMANCE FACTORS (WHAT YOU DO)

QUANTITY OF WORK: Your ability to produce needed work in appropriate amount to meet deadlines or satisfy objectives. The volume or number of work-related items you produce.

Possible examples of ratings may include:

❏ 5 = Outstanding	Almost always produces more than is required and delivers the work product ahead of schedule; assists others in completing their work.
❏ 4 = Exceeds Standards	Usually produces more than is required and is often ahead of schedule when delivering work products.
❏ 3 = Meets Standards	Produces an acceptable quantity of work as defined by the organization.
❏ 2 = Below Standards	Displays the ability to perform the job functions, but produces less than the desired quantity of output or misses deadlines because of work speed.
❏ 1 = Unacceptable	Usually produces less than the desired amount of work; does not meet the established minimum level of output; requires help to complete tasks.

Comments:

QUALITY OF WORK: The level of accuracy, appearance, or efficiency of your work output.

Possible examples of ratings may include:

❏ 5 = Outstanding	Produces work that is thorough and neat and contains exceptionally accurate information; performs work functions in an exemplary way that is a model for others; work samples are used as a model for others to follow.
❏ 4 = Exceeds Standards	Produces work that is thorough and neat; quality of work exceeds standards; produces high-quality work that saves money, time, or resources; receives customer compliments related to the quality of the work performed.
❏ 3 = Meets Standards	Produces an acceptable quality of work as defined by the supervisor and the job description; work is satisfactory, generally neat, and is usually without significant error.
❏ 2 = Below Standards	Displays the ability to perform the job functions, but produces less than the desired quality of output; produces work with errors or omissions.
❏ 1 = Unacceptable	Usually produces work with errors or omissions; responds to customer inquiries with incorrect information.

Comments:

JOB AND/OR TECHNICAL KNOWLEDGE: The level of job knowledge and/or skills you possess, in relation to your time in the position.

Possible examples of ratings may include:

❏ 5 = Outstanding	Teaches others to perform their job functions without being asked; understands and uses the historical perspectives relevant to the job to make the job more efficient; can be counted on to complete the work with excellent results.
❏ 4 = Exceeds Standards	Explains the job to other workers when asked; requires minimal supervision in order to complete the job properly.
❏ 3 = Meets Standards	Displays an acceptable level of job and/or technical knowledge and uses it appropriately to accomplish work tasks.
❏ 2 = Below Standards	Understands some, but not all of the basic principles of the job; requires additional supervision or help to complete the job properly.
❏ 1 = Unacceptable	Does not understand the basic principles of the job; unable to routinely perform the job effectively.

Comments:

ORAL AND WRITTEN COMMUNICATION: Your ability to express ideas, information, and/or instructions in a clear, organized, and concise manner. Your ability to express yourself in writing, when required by the job.

Possible examples of ratings may include:

❑ 5 = Outstanding	Written materials are error free; communication is concise and accurate; is used as a resource in communicating material to others.
❑ 4 = Exceeds Standards	Uses oral and written communication skills to foster positive working relationships; written material and/or oral presentations usually do not contain errors and are generally clear and easily understood.
❑ 3 = Meets Standards	Can express ideas verbally and in writing; errors in communication do not unduly hinder the recipient's understanding of the message.
❑ 2 = Below Standards	Written material requires more than one reading for clear understanding; oral communication leads to misunderstandings; difficulty in writing or speaking in a relevant or concise manner.
❑ 1 = Unacceptable	Written material and/or oral presentations are confusing and difficult to follow or understand; fails to record or recite pertinent information; oral communications lead to major miscommunications.

Comments:

COMPLIANCE WITH POLICIES: Your ability to understand, follow, and interpret company and work unit policies and rules. Such policies may include the operation and maintenance of work equipment and tools, attendance, compliance with Employee Handbook, or procedures and practices.

Possible examples of ratings may include:

❑ 5 = Outstanding	Actively supports all company and work unit policies, procedures, and rules; suggests new policies or rules that will enhance operations; proactively reports pertinent policy or procedure-related information with everyone they work with; always obtains the necessary approvals; regular and prompt in attendance; absences are planned and scheduled in advance.
❑ 4 = Exceeds Standards	Complies with all company rules, policies, and procedures, and often clarifies workplace rules for others; reports pertinent policy or procedure-related information in a timely manner; seeks supervisory approval whenever necessary; very prompt and regular in attendance; absences are infrequent and advance notice is given when time off is required.
❑ 3 = Meets Standards	Follows company and work unit rules, policies and procedures; follow procedures established for sharing and reporting information; seeks appropriate approvals where required; present and on time for each work shift; normally absences are preplanned and advance notice is given to the supervisor.

❏ 2 = Below Standards	Disregards company and work unit rules, policies, and procedures, but claims he/she was unaware of the policies; does not always share or report important policy or procedure-related information with the relevant parties; at times, does not seek necessary approvals; lax in attendance and/or reporting to work on time.
❏ 1 = Unacceptable	Violates company and work unit rules, policies and procedures, even when having been reminded of them; neglects to share or report important policy or procedure-related information with coworkers and/or supervisors that results in problems or mistakes; does not seek supervisory approval when required to do so; often absent without sufficient reason and/or frequently reports to work late or leaves early without prior notice.

Comments:

SECTION II: COMPANY VALUES (HOW YOU DO THE JOB)

SAFETY–Your ability to preserve the value of life and the environment.

Possible examples of ratings may include:

❏ 5 = Outstanding	Follows up on reported safety hazards to ensure problems have been corrected; makes safety-related suggestions to those who can make changes; looks out for the safety of others in the workplace.
❏ 4 = Exceeds Standards	Notices safety hazards and acts to correct them or reports them to the proper person; reports potential safety violations; actively promotes and demonstrates safety procedures, proper equipment utilization, and personal safety on the job.
❏ 3 = Meets Standards	Wears personal protective clothing, as required; follows safety-related operating procedures; observes safety practices throughout the workplace; uses equipment properly.
❏ 2 = Below Standards	Has been consulted about unsafe practices in the workplace; occasionally does not heed safety warnings or wear personal protective clothing, as required; uses equipment improperly.
❏ 1 = Unacceptable	Performs unsafe acts on the job that puts self and others at unnecessary risk; has repeated accidents; fails to follow accepted safety procedures; demonstrates disregard or negligence while operating equipment.

Comments:

PRIDE–You are enthusiastic and excited to produce extra effort and instill real quality in all you do.

Possible examples of ratings may include:

❏ 5 = Outstanding	Does more than is expected while promoting the company within the community; suggests improvements to the company's methods, even if suggestions impact functions outside of their work area; rarely needs supervisory follow-up; can be counted on to carry out complex instructions accurately; is a highly enthusiastic employee.
❏ 4 = Exceeds Standards	Shows initiative; suggests ways the workplace can be improved for everyone; requires little supervision; consistently follows instructions correctly; displays enthusiasm for the job; focuses on doing it right, not just on getting it done.
❏ 3 = Meets Standards	Produces work that is at the standard expected; is friendly in providing service to customers; shows responsiveness toward requests; works with minimum supervision; can be counted on to carry out assignments.
❏ 2 = Below Standards	Has difficulty following instructions; lacks diligence; work requires supervisory follow-up; displays a lack of interest in the job or in the goals of the company; cuts corners in order to complete a task.
❏ 1 = Unacceptable	Displays a lack of effort toward job duties; requires constant supervisory follow-up; his extreme difficulty following simple instructions; fails to seek clarification when confused.

Comments:

INNOVATION–Your ability to embrace each day's challenges as opportunities, with a spirit of creativity, resourcefulness, and an open mind. Your ability to adjust to changes in priorities, circumstances, direction, and personalities.

Possible examples of ratings may include:

❏ 5 = Outstanding	Makes suggestions for change within the workplace; looks for ways to enhance work processes; champions change; frequently demonstrates originality and aggressively seeks to resolve problems and pursue new ideas; demonstrates a positive approach to change and maximizes the opportunities created by change; consistently foresees needs and identifies possible solutions; consistently seeks job-related development.
❏ 4 = Exceeds Standards	Accepts reasonable changes; adjusts quickly to new priorities; suggests new ideas to help foster the change initiative; identifies problem areas and suggests or implements solutions, as practical; adjusts quickly to new priorities and helps foster acceptance in the workplace; pursues work and/or professional development.

❏ 3 = Meets Standards	Accepts reasonable change with occasional comments related to the change; may require some persuasion to adjust but generally adapts to workplace changes; aware of problem areas and attempts to solve problems with guidance from the supervisor; recognizes that change is part of the job and attempts to help foster changes in the workplace; pursues work-related development.
❏ 2 = Below Standards	Generally resists change; demonstrates a lack of understanding of reasonable changes being made in the workplace; displays resistance to changes that affect him/her personally; fails to foresee job-related needs; follows a routine way of performing job tasks without concern for improvement; limited job-related development.
❏ 1 = Unacceptable	Inflexible to changing circumstances; unable to respnd to day-to-day activities; unwilling to change; consistently inflexible to changing circumstances; shows no concern for work improvement of job-related development.

Comments:

RESPONSIBILITY–You are accountable for your words and actions, large and small. Your ability to recognize and identify job-related activity and to originate action.

Possible examples of ratings may include:

❏ 5 = Outstanding	Looks for ways to complete more tasks in less time; takes ownership for actions; looks for ways to correct mistakes and avoids them in the future; helps coworkers without being asked; requires little or no direction or supervision, even on nonroutine assignments.
❏ 4 = Exceeds Standards	Readily accepts new tasks not previously part of the job description; accepts new challenges with enthusiasm; recognizes when he/she has made mistakes; requires less than normal direction or supervision, even on nonroutine assignments.
❏ 3 = Meets Standards	Completes assigned work on time without being reminded; accepts responsibility for his/her work actions; does not gossip; requires normal direction and supervision on routine assignments; requires assistance on nonroutine assignments.
❏ 2 = Below Standards	Completes assigned tasks, but only after frequent reminders and supervisory follow-up; does not accept the outcome of his/her actions; spreads rumors and gossip; focuses on what others are doing or should do rather than concentrating on his/her own job duties and responsibilities.
❏ 1 = Unacceptable	Misses clearly established deadlines; doesn't fix mistakes or broken equipment; blames others for mistakes made on the job; initiates gossip or rumors; requires constant direction and supervision to complete assignments.

Comments:

TALK–Talk it out. Your ability to deal tactfully and effectively with others, especially when there is a difference of opinion. Your ability to work with and for others and in a team environment.

Possible examples of ratings may include:

❏ 5 = Outstanding	Facilitates the conflict resolution of others; initiates discussions in order to resolve workplace problems; is proactive in his/her communications; broadly influences others in a positive manner; even in stressful situations, fosters teamwork and positive relationships with everyone with whom they come in contact.
❏ 4 = Exceeds Standards	Foresees problems in order to prevent conflicts from occurring; fosters discussions to resolve issues before they become big; goes out of the way to cooperate and get along with others; shows genuine concern for others; works to develop rapport with others so that conflict can be resolved; expresses disagreement by offering productive alternatives.
❏ 3 = Meets Standards	Keeps relevant parties informed; discusses conflicts when asked to do so; seeks out information from others in order to do his/her job; expresses disagreement in a respectful manner; cooperative; gets along well with others; polite, courteous, and tactful; does not participate in conflict situations without attempting to resolve the differences.
❏ 2 = Below Standards	Avoids conflicts; does not reveal information that may be relevant to others; expresses disagreement in a way that does not respect others; helps others only when asked or pressured to do so; participates or contributes to conflict situations without working to resolve the differences.
❏ 1 = Unacceptable	Purposely hides important information; intentionally does not share thoughts or opinions; is unwilling to discuss conflicts or acknowledge their presence; demonstrates negativity toward work group members or toward the company goals; initiates conflict without the desire to resolve the differences; unwilling to assist peers or customers; frequently complains; not a team player.

Comments:

SECTION III: COMPLETION OF PROFESSIONAL DEVELOPMENT GOALS

Goals should be written in a specific, measurable, attainable, agreed upon, realistic, and time-oriented manner. Goals should include at least one opportunity for learning outside of normal job duties. (Attach a separate sheet, if more than 3 goals)

Development Goal Set Last Year	Result Achieved	Rank order goals in order of priority (1, 2, 3)	Affect overall rating? Y/N

SECTION IV: OVERALL PERFORMANCE RATING

❏ Outstanding	This rating means that you live and promote company values and that your performance throughout the rating period has been exceptional. This rating is usually reserved for employees who continue to excel in every area of the job or for those who have successfully completed unusually demanding special projects in addition to performing their regular duties.
❏ Exceeds Standards	This rating means that you are perceived as highly competent and recognizes that you do more than just meet the job requirements and do it well. You are also a strong proponent of the company's values. This rating should be perceived as a strong endorsement of your work.
❏ Meets Standards	This rating means that you are meeting the standards for the position and are doing a good job. You continue to support the company's values.
❏ Below Standards (Performance Improvement Plan recommended)	This rating means that performance is less than desired and improvement is required in work product or in upholding the company values. A Performance Improvement Plan can help you reach the company's desired performance.
❏ Unacceptable (Performance Improvement Plan required)	This rating means that your performance or your actions relative to the company's values are unacceptable and a Performance Improvement Plan and noticeable improvement is required to maintain your employment.

SECTION V: PROFESSIONAL DEVELOPMENT GOALS FOR NEXT YEAR

Goals should be written in a specific, measurable, attainable, agreed upon, realistic, and time-oriented manner. Goals should include at least one opportunity for learning outside of normal job duties. (Attach a separate sheet, if more than 3 goals)

Development Goals Planned for Next Year	Rank order goals in order of priority (1, 2, 3)	Affect overall rating? Y/N

SECTION VI: COMMENTS AND SIGNATURES

Supervisor's Comments (or attach additional page)

Employee's Comments (or attach additional page) Employee has five days to complete comments and may choose to write "no comment."

Action Taken:

❏ Merit Increase from $_____ to $_____ _____%
❏ Lump Sum Increase $_____ _____%
❏ Merit Increase Review Deferred _____ Days
❏ No Merit Increase
❏ Other: _____

Employee's signature:	Date:
Supervisor's signature:	Date:
Reviewer's signature:	Date:
Human resource staff signature:	Date:

Appeals: Employees may appeal overall performance ratings of "Unacceptable" or "Below Standards." Appeals should be submitted in writing to the reviewer within five business days of receiving the evaluation. The reviewer will consider the facts of the situation and respond to the employee in writing within ten business days of receiving the appeal. If the employee is not satisfied with the reviewer's decision on the appeal, the employee must then use the Grievance Procedure as outlined in the Personnel Rules.

APPENDIX: PERFORMANCE FACTORS FOR SUPERVISORS AND MANAGERS (WHAT SUPERVISORS DO)

MANAGERIAL EFFECTIVENESS/LEADERSHIP: Your ability to influence others and to provide effective direction in leadership situations. Your ability to coach, train, and develop employees' skills and abilities.

Possible examples of ratings may include:

❑ 5 = Outstanding	Inspires a high level of loyalty of employees evidenced by their commitment to excellence; uses innovative methods in giving direction and in motivating staff; considered an organizational leader and mentor; serves as a mentor in guiding employees to develop their job-related skills; advocates education and training for all employees.
❑ 4 = Exceeds Standards	Leads and develops strong teamwork; provides clear direction to others; appropriately allows them to make their own decisions and mistakes; offers suggestions and tools to help employees develop their skills and achieve their goals, including the development of personal action plans and written goal statements.
❑ 3 = Meets Standards	Works to develop a team; provides clear direction so that team members can be effective on the job; is respected as a leader; meets regularly with employees to discuss ways to develop their skills; knows the career aspirations of each employee.
❑ 2 = Below Standards	Provides limited direction to employees; employees do not work as a team; focused more on details or day-to-day operations rather than motivating staff to do so; assists some employees in reaching their career goals; does not meet regularly or consistently with employees to discuss their development; closely manages employee work performance without giving room for employees to learn as they work.
❑ 1 = Unacceptable	Causes employee dissatisfaction; does not provide direction to others, even when asked to do so; does not assist employees in developing their skills; is unaware of developmental opportunities for employees within and outside of the company.

Comments:

DECISION MAKING: Your ability to analyze and interpret information and arrive at logical conclusions in a timely manner, within established policies.

Possible examples of ratings may include:

❏ 5 = Outstanding	Innovative decision-maker regardless of complexity; confident under pressure; considers long- and short-term consequences; assists others in decision making; uses the company values to guide decisions.
❏ 4 = Exceeds Standards	Evaluates data quickly and accurately; logical conclusions supported by facts; foresees potential problems and considers alternatives; considers the company values when making decisions.
❏ 3 = Meets Standards	Able and willing to make appropriate decisions within an appropriate time frame; analyzes facts and draws conclusions in a satisfactory manner; considers impacts of decisions on other work areas; acknowledges the company values when making decisions.
❏ 2 = Below Standards	Demonstrates little confidence in own decision-making ability; decisions may not be arrived at in a timely manner; impacts of decisions may not be considered thoroughly.
❏ 1 = Unacceptable	Unwilling and/or relies on others to make decisions; decisions are frequently incorrect or not based on facts; decisions adversely affect other work areas.

Comments:

PLANNING, PRIORITIZING, AND DELEGATING: Your ability to develop goals and objectives and identify the resources needed; the use of time and the delegation of human resources and equipment or facilities to meet predetermined deadline. Your ability to identify and assign appropriate work tasks to others.

Possible examples of ratings may include:

❏ 5 = Outstanding	Innovative planning providing for effective uses of resources; organizational and departmental goals integrated to enhance project results; reprioritizes to meet unforeseen circumstances; typically delegates both responsibility and authority with challenging tasks to others; provides training, if necessary.
❏ 4 = Exceeds Standards	Thorough planning with insight into future needs; assists in department's goal setting; prioritizes work and is often ahead of schedule; creates SMAART goals for each employee; frequently assigns appropriate work tasks to others to meet goals and objectives and promotes growth.

❏ 3 = Meets Standards	Reasonable and sufficient planning to meet project needs; goals consistent with organization's; priorities set to meet important deadlines; correctly identifies and assigns appropriate work tasks to be handled by others and establishes appropriate deadlines for completion.
❏ 2 = Below Standards	Inadequate preparation for projects; sometimes overlooks organization's goals; sometimes fails to meet deadlines; takes on additional tasks that interfere with the workload; assigns wrong work tasks or fails to assign work tasks to others.
❏ 1 = Unacceptable	Does not plan ahead or consider organization's goals; work effort disorganized; insufficient time available for priorities; deadlines not met; unable to identify appropriate work tasks for others or does not delegate.

Comments:

EFFECTIVE USE OF PERFORMANCE EVALUATIONS: Your ability to prepare and carry out employee evaluations in a productive and timely manner.

Possible examples of ratings may include:

❏ 5 = Outstanding	Uses the evaluation process to motivate employees and as a career development tool; clearly expresses performance expectations and indicates on the evaluation when the employee has met those exceptions; completes performance evaluations on time or ahead of schedule.
❏ 4 = Exceeds Standards	Uses the evaluation process as a developmental tool for employees; performance evaluations are complete and on time and indicate that they were prepared mutually with the employee; expectations for performance are clear to all employees.
❏ 3 = Meets Standards	Performance evaluations are completed on time; performance expectations for employees are clear; employees' goals are SMAART.
❏ 2 = Below Standards	Performance evaluations are typically not completed on time; documentation is not complete; employees are confused about performance expectations or complain that expectations are not clear; employee goals are not specific or measurable.
❏ 1 = Unacceptable	Performance evaluations are not timely and/or accurate; does not keep appropriate documentation; does not communicate performance expectations to employees; employees do not have SMAART performance goals.

Comments:

PERFORMANCE IMPROVEMENT PLAN

Use this form to provide additional guidance to an employee who needs to improve an area of their performance.

Employee Name: _____

Job Title: _____

Supervisor: _____

Department: _____

<u>Directions:</u> A Performance Improvement Plan is required for rating factors rated "Unacceptable" and is recommended for rating factors rated "Below Standards." The supervisor should prepare the Performance Improvement Plan, with involvement from the reviewer. The purpose of the plan is to help the employee improve in areas noted as deficient on the Performance Evaluation Form. The plan is to specify areas for improvement, identify activities designed to strengthen the employee's performance, and indicate expected outcomes. A separate form can be used for each area requiring improvement, or all areas may be listed on one form.

Areas of Improvement:
1.
2.
3.
4.

Activities Designed to Improve Performance:
1.
2.
3.
4.

Expected Performance Outcomes and Completion Dates:
1.
2.
3.
4.

Timeline for Improvement:
Date this performance plan begins:
Check-in dates:

Required Signatures:

Employee's signature:	Date:
Supervisor's signature:	Date:
Reviewer's signature:	Date:
Human resource staff signature:	Date:

Distribution: Employee　　　　Supervisor　　　　HR-Personnel File

Index